ARBITRATION

A Practical Guide

DEDICATED
WITH AFFECTION AND RESPECT
TO THE MEMORY

OF

SIR JOHN LAING CBE
(1879–1978)

FROM WHOM
I LEARNED A GREAT DEAL

Arbitration

A Practical Guide

Arthur T. Ginnings
FRICS FCIArb FBIM

Gower

© Arthur T. Ginnings 1984

All rights reserved. No part of this publication may be reproduced, stored in a retrieval system, or transmitted in any form or by any means, electronic, mechanical, photocopying, recording, or otherwise without the prior permission of Gower Publishing Company Limited.

Published by
Gower Publishing Company Limited
Aldershot, Hants, England

British Library Cataloguing in Publication Data

Ginnings, Arthur T.
Arbitration.
1. Arbitration and award—England
I. Title
344.207'9 KD7645

ISBN 0-566-02423-3

Printed in Great Britain by
Redwood Burn Limited, Trowbridge, Wiltshire
Typeset by Guildford Graphics Limited, Guildford, Surrey

Contents

Foreword

by John J. L. Corkill, FSVA, FRSH, FIB, FCIArb
President (1975–76) (now Chartered) Institute of Arbitrators

'They who in quarrels interpose
Must often wipe a bloody nose'
(John Gay: 1685–1732)

This saying is often true about anyone who becomes involved in other parties' quarrels. It does not apply normally to arbitrators who are called in to settle disputes although it might if the arbitrator does not adhere to the basic rules and, above all, to the basic principles which to a large extent make arbitration preferable to litigation.

Arbitration procedures have been changing in recent years probably far more rapidly than ever before – not only because of the ever widening international scene and the need for low cost schemes, but also in the nature and spread of the fields covered. Changes necessitate up-to-date information and any new book which throws further light on the subject is welcome. The author of this book amply fulfils this task and, because he brings to it experience of an administrative role in arbitration as well as the knowledge required of an arbitrator, the book is of especial value to the practitioner and student alike. One of the attributes of modern arbitration, particularly in the small claims and consumer fields, is simplicity. Mr Ginnings has without losing effect set out clearly and in readily understood terms the advantages of arbitration, its basis, the procedures and the help that can be offered both to experienced and 'beginner' arbitrators and, perhaps above all, to the parties. It is important that arbitration is understood by laymen, corporate or individual, who look to this form of settlement especially when there is need to avoid publicity. This publication is admirable for anyone in this category. Particularly, I feel, the definition of basic terms and phrases is a very useful part of the book since a large number of the terms used are rarely understood properly by all concerned. The future of arbitration belongs to those who can best adapt to change and the author has set an example to others in bringing modern thought to this very old method of settling disputes. He is to be congratulated on the clarity and human feeling he has brought to the task.

Do not pervert justice; do not show partiality to the poor or favouritism to the great, but judge your neighbour fairly.

Jehovah
(Leviticus 19:15—NIV)

It is not merely of some importance but is of fundamental importance that justice should not only be done, but should manifestly and undoubtedly be seen to be done.

Lord Hewart (1870–1943)
In *R. v. Sussex Justices* (1923)

Preface

The practice of arbitration has emerged from historic and socio-political developments as an important aspect of commercial life in many countries so that now, increasingly, parties to transactions in commerce and industry stipulate that any dispute arising from such dealings will be settled by arbitration and, to give effect to that intention, an appropriate provision is incorporated in their contracts.

Commercial arbitration, it must be emphasised, is not *mediation* or *conciliation.* The former could be described as an informal process resulting in a formal but non-binding recommendation by a third party; the latter is an attempt to persuade the parties to reach a settlement by mutual agreement; but, in any such circumstances, if either party resiles, no agreement can be enforced. Arbitration results in an independent decision by a third party which, whether they like it or not, the disputing parties have agreed to accept. Thus, an essential pre-requisite in arbitration is an agreement between the parties that the arbitrator's decision will be accepted as final and binding. Even so, there is sometimes considerable reluctance by the 'losing' party to accept the finality of any such imposed decision and, in those circumstances, the 'successful' party can seek enforcement through the court.

Another important distinction to be kept in mind is the fundamental difference between commercial arbitration and the more widely publicised arbitration procedure applied to industrial disputes – to which further reference is made in Chapter 10.

What is more, human nature being what it is, disputes between individuals and groups are, and will continue to be, a feature of every-day life in all sections of society – even, unfortunately, when one or both parties are professing Christians. In these last-mentioned circumstances, those concerned can and should be guided by the clear teaching of the New Testament* from which the following procedure emerges:

(i) Do your best to get the matter settled by mutual agreement between the parties; then, if that proves to be impossible –

*Matthew 18:15–17; 1 Corinthians 6:1–8.

(ii) Get the matter ventilated before witnesses with the same object; then, if that proves to be impossible –
(iii) Tell it to the church to have the matter decided and settled; then, if that proves to be impossible –
(iv) Inform the recalcitrant party (or parties) that he (or they) have forfeited the sympathy and respect of fellow-Christians until the matter has been put right.

A question will doubtless arise with regard to the meaning of 'tell it to the church' and it is suggested that –

(i) in respect of disputes between members of one group or congregation it means –
(a) informing the leaders of that body – who may be able to deal with certain situations without undue publicity; and/or,
(b) involving the whole congregation as may be necessary.
(ii) in respect of disputes between members of separate groups the leaders and/or members of all groups concerned should be similarly informed.
(iii) when a dispute and its potential repercussions are such as to affect a wide cross-section of church members the solution of the matter could be referred to a properly set up arbitration process operated under Christian principles.

By means of arbitration, the matter(s) in dispute can be settled with the minimum of formality and without publicity, albeit with the option of applying to the court for an enforcement order if that should become necessary.

It is appreciated that countless numbers of problems are dealt with every day on the basis of person-to-person care and counselling. Not every problem is amenable to being dealt with by that means, however, and it would be helpful to those concerned to know that suitably qualified and experienced men and women are available to assist the parties in disputes – either as counsellors, conciliators or arbitrators – according to their needs and wishes.

Purpose of the Book

So, the primary purpose of this book is to provide in simple and jargon-free terms, a general idea of what arbitration is and how it works. Secondly, it indicates how and where advice and services in connection with arbitration can be obtained and, thirdly, it contains information and guidance about procedures for the benefit of those who appreciate the availability of a compact reference source as and when the need arises.

For the author, the present work has been an enjoyable scramble among the foothills of arbitration while leaving the higher and more inaccessible peaks unscaled. There can be no more appropriate way to conclude these preliminary comments than by quoting from the introduction to '*A New and Complete Law-Dictionary*' published in 1764:

> Nothing more need be faid in favour of the work propofed: it remainf only to fee, in what manner it will be executed, and in what refpect it will be more ufeful than, or preferable to, the other performances of a fimilar nature that have been publifhed. . . . But tho' he [the author] is determined to exert the utmost degree of patience and industry he is mafter of in making this work ufeful; yet he is fo far from being vain of his own abilities, that any hint for improving it, either in form or fubstance, communicated to him by any perfon whatfoever, will be thankfully received and gratefully acknowledged.

And that (subject to up-dating the style!) is precisely how I wish to present this work.

Eastbourne
December 1983

ARTHUR T. GINNINGS

Acknowledgements

The help and encouragement I have received from others – too numerous to mention comprehensively – is gratefully acknowledged. In particular, I wish to place on record my indebtedness to J. J. L. Corkhill FSVA, FRSH, FIB, P/PCIArb, for contributing the Foreword, to J. Verdin Davis, Barrister, FCIArb and Robert J. Wren FRICS, FIAS, ACIArb, MCSI, for perusing the draft and making suggestions for improving it, to Allan G. Houston FRICS, FCIArb, for some notes and comments on the arbitration process under Scottish Law, to S. P. Finn Esq. for directing my attention to the story of the *Ouzel*, to the Chartered Institute of Arbitrators for the help derived from its publications and services, to the Librarian of the City of London Guildhall Library, for affording access to the Arbitration Acts of 1698 and 1889, to Mrs Olwyn Llewellyn for her competence and patience in typing (and retyping) the text and, especially, to Amy, my wife, for her role of 'study widow' during many hours while this and other writing was in progress and, subsequently, for reading and checking the printed text.

A.T.G.

PART I
ARBITRATION IN PRACTICE

1 Arbitration and the Law

Common Law and Contract

Before reviewing some of the legal instruments which exist to support and regulate arbitration proceedings, it may be worth reminding ourselves that English people live under a 'common law' system. This bestows certain rights and duties upon every individual and includes the application of the law of tort to the right of any person to recover any loss or damage he suffers which is held to have been caused by another party with whom he has no contractual relationship. A contract may to some extent modify the application of common law to a particular situation but, unless it is so limited, common law is always there to protect and control members of society as and when necessary.

Common law has its roots in 'natural justice' and has developed from primitive societies where the universal customs of the realm, being a reflection of social attitudes, become the 'common law'. What is generally held to be 'fair and reasonable' or 'just and equitable' are the conceptual foundations for common law. The English common law system developed progressively from the period following the Norman conquest and, at the same time, owes something to the earlier influence of the Romans who had established their rule of law in the territories which came under their jurisdiction.

In its application to particular situations, common law has been extended and clarified by decisions of the courts down the years which, collectively, become 'case law' – based on the principle that previous decisions become precedents on which future cases are decided. Consequently, a good deal of time in the courts can be taken up by argument whether a previous judgment in one case or another should or should not govern the decision in a current dispute.

As mentioned, common law rights can be overruled by specific contracts and most of us are familiar with various sorts of document having conditions printed or referred to therein (sometimes readable only with the aid of a magnifying glass) which, if studied carefully, could be found to affect one's general rights under common law. Anyone wanting to buy a particular product may be able to do so only on the basis of certain standard conditions of trading and, unless one agrees to buy on those conditions, no sale will normally be effected.

Today, there is a considerable amount of legislation under which a 'consumer' is given a great deal more protection than he previously had under so-called 'guarantees'. Such legislation, in effect, overrides any exclusion clause which purports to deprive a purchaser of his common law rights. Purchasers of a new appliance who are urged to complete and return a guarantee card would be well advised not to do so. The customer could have thus agreed, for example, that while the replacement of defective parts is free he (the customer) will pay for all associated labour and carriage costs.

The construction industry operated for many years 'The National Schedule of Daywork Charges' until the Restrictive Practices Court ruled that document to be against the public interest. It not only defined 'prime cost' but also prescribed the percentage additions thereto for overheads and profit and this meant that the employer (customer) had no option but to pay for 'daywork' on that basis. Nowadays, the industry uses the same sort of document to define 'prime cost' but without prescribing any percentage addition. Moreover, the current document is not a unilateral publication.

These examples illustrate the way in which general rights under common law can be trimmed and even extinguished by contract. It is only fair to add that all is not always sinister; there is nothing wrong in two consenting parties entering into any contract – provided that it is not in itself illegal – and there is nothing to stop their agreeing to be bound by whatever conditions they wish to incorporate in any such agreement. Injustice occurs only when one party is in a monopolistic situation and imposes on the other party, who is in a weaker position, conditions which are not equitable. It is worth noting, in this context, that the application of the Unfair Contract Terms Act 1977 is not limited to transactions in which one of the parties is a 'consumer'.

Essential Ingredients of a Valid Contract

To be enforceable by law, an agreement must

1 be legal;
2 define what is offered by whom and to whom;
3 express the acceptance of such offer by the party or parties to whom it is made;
4 define any governing provisions, and
5 (if 'under hand') define the related 'consideration'.

For obvious reasons, it is preferable for any such agreement to be confirmed in writing – either by the exchange of letters or by means of a properly executed memorandum – but contracts made orally are also valid.

Statute Law: England and Wales

The first English statute enacted to govern and support arbitrations was the Arbitration Act 1698. From this it can be seen that many of the basic concepts incorporated in current legislation have their roots in the past. Arbitrations in England and Wales are currently governed by the Arbitration Act 1950 as amended and extended by the Acts of 1975 and 1979. Copies of these Acts are obtainable from Her Majesty's Stationery Office (government book shops) and are also reproduced as appendixes in certain textbooks. This book includes a 'Lay-man's Guide' to each of these Acts in Part II. The 1950 Act repealed the Arbitration Act 1934 and other related legislation going back to and including the Arbitration Act 1894. The Arbitration Act 1975 gives qualified effect in the UK to the 1958 New York Convention on the Recognition and Enforcement of Foreign Arbitral Awards, and also amends the 1950 Act to the extent necessary to remove any conflict between it and the 1975 Act; it came into operation on 23 December 1975 and the UK thus became the seventy-third state to associate itself with that Convention. The Convention to which it is related was adopted by the United Nations Conference on International Commercial Arbitration on 10 June 1958. The 1979 Act is a reforming measure, as more fully explained below, and came into effect on 1 August 1979. An amendment to S.1 and S.2 thereof is made by S.148 of the Supreme Court Act 1981.

Many other statutes, about sixty in England/Wales and another dozen or so in Scotland, also provide for arbitration. The Agricultural Holdings Act 1948 and the London Building Acts 1930–9 are examples of such statutes – the latter being the legal basis on which party-wall disputes/awards in London are dealt with. Others include legislation with regard to compensation for the compulsory purchase of land and property, while similar provisions exist with regard to compensation for personal injury under legislation dealing with workmen's compensation and employer's liability. Such arbitrations are referred to as 'statutory arbitrations' to distinguish them from others which could be referred to as 'voluntary arbitrations'.

The Arbitration Act 1950

One important feature of the 1950 Act is the provision under S.4 whereby if either party to an arbitration agreement initiates court proceedings against the other, the party sued can apply to the court for, and will normally be granted, a stay of such court proceedings on the ground that the parties are bound by an arbitration agreement – provided that he has not condoned those proceedings by entering a defence or otherwise. In the event that a stay is granted, the court proceedings are thereupon suspended – and this applies in the County Court as well as in the High Court. If, however, the existence and/or nature of such arbitration agreement is challenged, the court may refuse to allow a stay of judicial proceedings. This illustrates how the Act gives an arbitration agreement its 'bite' and why, so often, people who may have preferred to proceed in the courts are hamstrung by the fact that litigation can be barred when an arbitration agreement exists between them and another party. However, S.24(2) of the 1950 Act enables the court to set aside an arbitration agreement when any related allegation of fraud is referred to it. This also demonstrates how the court is always there, albeit in the background, and can be requested as and when appropriate to regulate or reinforce any arbitration proceedings. It is also worth emphasising that the court will not interfere unless asked to do so by one or more of the parties or the arbitrator or umpire concerned.

'Special Case' Procedure under the 1950 Act

Perhaps the most dramatic provision of the 1979 Act is S.1(1) which repeals S.21 of the 1950 Act – under which the famous 'Case Stated' or 'Special Case' procedure was operated for many years. It also removes from the court power to remit or set aside an award merely because of an error of fact or of law on the face of it. Instead, parties now have a limited right of appeal to the court on any question of law arising from an award provided that all parties concur in such appeal or, alternatively, by leave of the court. Such leave cannot be given unless the question raised is deemed by the court to be one that could substantially effect the rights of the parties. Then, if such leave is given, the court may impose conditions – such as the payment into court of the damages specified in the award. In any case, it should be noted that the time within which any such appeal can be made is now 21 days from publication of the award in question. (See (15), Part III.)

The Arbitration Act 1975

A guide to the 1975 Act is given in Part II. It is not otherwise dealt with in this book because, being related to the complexities of international commercial arbitration, it is beyond the capacity of the average non-specialist to enter upon it – in theory or in practice – without the aid of a legal expert.

The Arbitration Act 1979

One of the declared purposes of the 1979 Act was to encourage the return of foreign disputes to the English arbitration scene. Its provisions are detailed in

Part II but it may be helpful to focus attention here on the main changes to previous English practice permitted or made necessary by its provisions. This Act received Royal Assent on 4 April 1979 (on the eve of the dissolution of Parliament) and came into operation on 1 August 1979 subject to the proviso that proceedings commenced before that date were exempted unless the parties agreed otherwise.

Questions of Law Under the 1979 Act

The 1979 Act provides for a limited right of appeal to the court on points of law. In practice, this limitation may prove to be no more than a means of 'screening' by the court to ensure that the genuineness of all such submissions is tested and thereby prevented from becoming merely a delaying tactic. The right of appeal from the High Court to the Court of Appeal is also restricted for similar reasons. Otherwise, subject to the granting of the necessary leave, the procedure for obtaining a decision by the court on a point of law under the 1979 Act remains broadly the same as it was under the 1950 Act.

It is not only for academic interest, therefore, that a note on the special case procedure is included as (15) in Part III; it could also be used as a guide to a submission under the provisions of S.2 of the 1979 Act – subject as therein provided.

If the parties have excluded their right of appeal by means of a valid exclusion agreement they will have agreed, in effect, that the arbitrator's decision in that case is conclusive both as to fact and law. In such circumstances, the arbitrator's decision cannot be challenged and the proceedings cannot be thus prolonged.

Reasons

Another significant innovation is the qualified provision whereby the court, before giving its ruling on any such appeal, may order the arbitrator to supply the reasons for his award or any part of it. This cannot be so ordered, however, unless it is established that at least one of the parties gave prior notice that a reasoned award was required or there was good reason why no such notice was given.

Appeals from decisions of the court are also limited by the 1979 Act. These can now be made only if the court or the Court of Appeal (CA) gives leave to do so and it is certified by the court that the subject of any such appeal is of such importance to the general public or otherwise that it merits consideration by the CA.

Freedom of Parties to Agree Procedure

As in respect of any agreement, the parties thereto can further agree to modify or extinguish it – or, merely, to ignore it. Thus, the parties could concur in referring a particular question to the court despite their previous agreement not to do so – and vice versa. A further provision of the 1979 Act is the freedom of the parties to agree procedural arrangements which could otherwise have been an improper attempt to oust the jurisdiction of the court. In particular, parties are permitted to enter into an 'exclusion agreement' whereby they abandon even their limited rights of access to the court as previously mentioned. It must be noted, however, that no such exclusion agreement can be made until after a dispute has actually arisen; nor, in any case, in relation to any statutory arbitration proceedings. Otherwise, the jurisdiction of the court remains unimpaired.

Exclusion Clauses

The following is a typical exclusion clause as issued by the Chartered Institute of Arbitrators for incorporation in correspondence, or other written documents exchanged by the parties, thereby creating a valid exclusion agreement related to domestic arbitration: *'If and in so far as English law applies to the arbitration hereby agreed, the parties further agree to exclude any right of application or appeal to the English courts in connection with any question of law arising in the course of the reference or out of the Award'.*

An alternative form of such an exclusion agreement was published as N.L.J. Precedent No. 297 in *New Law Journal* (20 September 1979).

Delays

Arbitrators have no power to act as can a judge in dismissing an action for want of prosecution but, under S.5 of the 1979 Act, they can apply to the court for such an extension of their basic powers as may be appropriate and necessary to deal with inordinate delay by a party in arbitration proceedings. Even so, parties who directly or indirectly condone such delay may not find the court to be automatically in sympathy with any such application. In his speech to the House of Lords in *Bremer Vulkan Schiffbau und Maschinenfabrik* v. *South India Corporation Ltd (1981)*, Lord Diplock said: *'Respondents in private arbitrations are not entitled to let sleeping dogs lie and then complain that they did not bark.'*

Other 'hold-ups' which could occur under previous legislation, and which the 1979 Act is designed to overcome, include the timing of the appointment of an umpire (in a two-arbitrator-plus-umpire reference) and failure by a third party named as the appointing/nominating authority in an arbitration agreement to act accordingly.

Consumer Protection

General legislation previously referred to in the 'consumer' field includes the Consumer Protection Act 1971, the Hire Purchase Act 1965, the Trade Descriptions Act 1968, the Fair Trading Act 1973, the Supply of Goods (Implied Terms) Act 1973, the Consumer Credit Act 1974, the Restrictive Trade Practices Act 1976, the Unfair Contract Terms Act 1977 (UCTA), the Sale of Goods Act 1979, the Estate Agents Act 1979 and the Competition Act 1980. All this has followed and, to some extent, amends the famous Sale of Goods Act 1893. The enforcement of such legislation is the duty of the Office of Fair Trading (O.F.T.) set up under S.1 of the Fair Trading Act 1973. Accordingly, 'consumers' are much better protected than they were before the current legislation was enacted. It is of interest to note in passing the opinion of the then Lord Chief Justice that, in respect of the Trade Descriptions Act 1968, a builder supplies 'services' rather than 'goods' *(Beckett* v. *Cohen: 1972).*

A 'consumer' is defined by S.12 of UCTA as, in effect, a party to a contract who does not enter into that contract in the course of his normal business while the other party does so. Furthermore, to be regarded as a 'consumer' in a transaction which involves the passing of goods, the purchaser must be seen to be acquiring such goods for private use or consumption.

UCTA became effective in February 1978 and, as such, is one of several measures enacted in recent years to protect ordinary men and women against many of the risks to which they were previously exposed as a consequence of their ignorance or folly in entering into various sorts of contract or agreement for the supply of goods and/or services. This Act empowers judges and arbitrators to set aside any clause which is held not to be fair or reasonable in any contract to which a consumer is a party and, for that purpose, defines in S.11 what has become known as 'the test of reasonableness'. This is 'that the term shall have been a fair and reasonable one to be included having regard to the circumstances which were, or ought reasonably to have been, known to or in the contemplation of the parties when the contract was made'. The section also provides that it is for those claiming that a contract term or notice satisfies the requirement of reasonableness to show that it does so. Consequently, it seems likely that clauses designed to exclude or limit the liability of the supplier in respect of goods/services he supplies may fail the 'reasonableness test'. Other important provisions of UCTA have to be observed but it should be noted that the following categories of contract are excluded from the scope of SS.2–3–4–7 as detailed in Schedule 1 of the Act

(a) contracts of insurance;
(b) contracts to create, transfer or extinguish an interest in
  (i) land,
  (ii) technical/commercial 'know-how';
(c) contracts related to certain company affairs; and
(d) contracts related to certain transactions in securities.

Institutional Arbitrations

One effect of such consumer legislation is that arbitration provisions are being incorporated in the standard conditions of trading of an increasing number of trade associations – under the persuasive pressure of the OFT. This has led to the increasing use of arbitration for the settlement of disputes in the consumer field in general. Furthermore, trade associations concerned in the supply of particular goods and services have set up special low-cost schemes which provide for the settlement of disputes by arbitration when other means have failed. Such special schemes are in the nature of 'institutional arbitrations' and each of them is governed by particular rules approved by the OFT. Of these, the schemes operated by the National House-Building Council (NH-BC), the Association of British Travel Agents (ABTA), the Society of Motor Manufacturers and Traders (SMMT), the Motor Agents Association (MAA) and others mentioned in Chapter 11 are becoming widely known and used.

Small Claims

Subject to certain exclusions, S.39 of the County Courts Act 1959 ('the 1959 Act') provides that claims under contract and in tort for amounts not exceeding £2000 can be settled by the County Court. Furthermore, an arbitration procedure is quite often adopted in the County Court for the settlement of 'small claims' (say under £500) and, in particular, those under £200, when it is not necessary for the Registrar to obtain the consent of *both* parties before proceeding on that basis. Even so, the very idea of going to court is enough, in many cases, to inhibit an otherwise justified claim from being pursued in that manner or at all.

'Outside Arbitrators' in County Courts

Under S.92 of the 1959 Act it is provided that particular matters may be referred to an 'outside arbitrator' – that is to say, a person (other than the judge or registrar of that court) who possesses some special skill or other expertise and acts, more or less, as would an 'Official Referee' or, since 1975, a Judge–Arbitrator in the High Court. His award becomes, in effect, a judgment of the County Court in the case concerned. Such arbitration proceedings are conducted in private and relatively informally and, if oral evidence is given, the strict rules of evidence are not necessarily enforced. Furthermore, with the consent of the parties, an expert can be engaged to give independent evidence or, as another option, the case can be dealt with on the basis of written submissions and documentary evidence alone. In other respects, the arbitrator is also free to adopt any procedure which he considers to be convenient and fair to both parties. On the other hand, if it becomes necessary, the arbitrator can proceed on an *'ex parte'* basis. The costs of the action up to and including the entry of judgment are in the discretion of the arbitrator equally as of the court under the provisions of the County Court Rules. Under Order 37 Rule 7 of those rules, any application to have an arbitrator's award under S.92 set aside must be made to the County Court within six days of receipt by the party concerned of a copy of the relative judgment. There is no appeal against the arbitrator's findings as such. The only grounds on which the judge or registrar can consider setting aside an award are that the arbitrator had no jurisdiction, that he demonstrated his personal bias or that an error of law is evident on the face of it. Should the judge or registrar dismiss such an application an appeal may be made to the Court of Appeal subject as provided in S.108 of the 1959 Act.

S.7(3) of the 1979 Act excludes the application of the provisions of S.31 of the 1950 Act to proceedings under S.92 of the 1959 Act. That is to say, proceedings under S.92 of the 1959 Act are not 'statutory arbitrations' under S.31 of the 1950 Act.

An outside arbitrator appointed under County Court arbitration rules can be any person who is suitable and who agrees to act in that manner. He will normally be paid a fee for his services and the Clerk of the Court will require a deposit by the parties to cover such fees/expenses as the arbitrator may require. This factor could be a disincentive to the adoption of this procedure but, whatever the reasons, it seems that the provisions of S.92 are seldom invoked in some County Courts. If no outside arbitrator has been requested by the parties either the judge or the registrar of the court can act as arbitrator under the same rules. All this, and a great deal more, is fully explained in the booklet *Small Claims in the County Court* – see Bibliography.

Local Small Claims Courts

Typical of other experiments in the establishment of less cumbersome and, consequently, less awe-inspiring means of dealing with small claims in a judicial manner was the Westminster Small Claims Court (WSCC) established by the City of Westminster Law Society in association with the National Association of Citizen's Advice Bureaux, the Consumer's Association and Westminster City Council. That service was disbanded in 1979 but it is of interest to note that disputes about claims for amounts between £10 and £250 could be submitted under that scheme to WSCC provided the court Administrator was satisfied that the applicant had taken all steps reasonably necessary to settle the matter. If so, the dispute was referred by the Administrator to an Adjudicator appointed by the President of the City of Westminster Law Society to deal with the matter. The relatively simple procedure of preparing and answering the claim was supervised by the Administrator up to the point at which the case went before the Adjudicator who could, if necessary, invite the parties to appear at a semi-formal 'hearing' which was not subject to the usual rules of evidence. The final decision of the Adjudicator was made binding upon the parties by relating it to the Arbitration Act 1950. As to costs, the plaintiff paid a fee of £5 (£10 if the claim exceeded £100) but this could be wholly or partly waived in certain circumstances. The same applied in respect of any counter-claim. In addition to giving his/her decision about the amount in dispute, the Adjudicator could order either party to reimburse the fee paid by the other party plus a sum (not normally exceeding £10) towards the court's expenses. These and other details of the WSCC service are now only of academic interest since, as already mentioned, it was disbanded in 1979. They are included as a further example of the sort of procedures that can be adopted, by agreement of the parties, in the settlement of disputes by arbitration.

The Limitation Acts

The Limitation Act 1939 replaced previous legislation including the famous Statute of Limitations 1623 and the Civil Procedure Act 1883.

As far as arbitration is concerned, the significance of the 1939 Act is the time limit it imposes on the bringing of actions in commercial disputes. Putting it another way, actions must be brought within a limited period after the date on which 'the cause of the action' accrued. So, what determines that date? In respect of a dispute it is the date when the claimant first acquired the right of action and, in respect of an award, it is the date of the award. For contracts 'under hand' such limit is six years; in the case of contracts 'under seal' (deeds) the period is twelve years.

Actions initiated outside those periods can be 'estopped' (meaning 'stopped') as being 'Statute Barred'. This is an adequate defence. Sometimes, a question about the time limit can be critical and, if such is the case, the Act provides that an arbitration is deemed to commence when one party serves a notice on the other requiring him to concur in the appointment of an arbitrator. So, provided that such a move occurs within the six-year or the twelve-year period, as may be appropriate, the Limitation Act will not apply.

When does a Cause of Action 'Accrue'?

It is important to note, that in *Sparham-Souter and Another* v. *Town and Country Developments (Essex) Limited, and Benfleet Urban District Council* (1976) the Court of Appeal reversed a decision in a previous case and declared that a person's cause of action does not 'accrue' under the Limitation Act 1939 until he is in a position to discover the relevant facts – in that case, defects in a building.

It has also been held that the date on which the prescribed time-limit begins to run may be postponed on account of disability, fraudulent concealment or error. On the other hand, such time will run in respect of a debt from the date of a part payment or a written and signed acknowledgement of the plaintiff's title.

Questions may arise about third-party claims brought against one party to a contract in respect of which he is indemnified by another party under the provisions of that contract – for example, by the sort of indemnity given by the contractor to the employer under clause 20 of the J.C.T. 1980 Standard Form of Building Contract. In *Green and Silley Weir* v. *British Railways Board* (1980) it was decided by Mr Justice Dillon that the Board was not 'statute barred' in respect of its claim to be indemnified by a contractor (Kavanagh) against, *inter alia,* claims under a clause in an agreement between the Board and the contractor – despite the fact that more than six years had elapsed since the damage complained of had occurred. The main reasoning behind this decision appears to be that the time-limit in these circumstances did not begin to run until the Board's liability to the third-party had been established and quantified.

Industrial injury disputes are mainly outside the scope of this book but it may be of interest to mention that the Limitation Act 1975 amends the time within which actions may be commenced in respect of personal injury or death under the legislation related to master/servant relationships. The statutory period of three years is not itself altered but it now runs from either

(a) the date on which the cause of the action accrued; or,
(b) the date of the plaintiff's knowledge of the relevant facts; or,
(c) in cases of fatal accidents, (i) the date of death or (ii) the date of knowledge of the relevant facts by the person for whom the action is brought – whichever is the later.

Want of Prosecution

Although not related to the legislation mentioned above, there is another sort of limitation which, in certain circumstances, could be applied. This is by an application to have a case 'struck out' from the court list 'for want of prosecution'. In court proceedings, the grounds for such an application would have to show clearly that the plaintiff had not complied with the Rules of the Supreme Court with regard to the time factor prescribed by those Rules and the Orders made thereunder. For example, Order 25, Rule 1(1)(b) provides for the court to give directions at an early stage as to the future course of the action and it is incumbent upon the plaintiff to motivate such directions by an appropriate application. The Court of Appeal decided in *Renown Investments and Others* v. *F. Shepherd and Others* (1976) that a 'no-action' period of about two and a half years was inexcusable in the circumstances of that case and allowed it to be struck out for that reason.

The same principle was applied in two other cases – *Gregg and Others* v. *Raytheon Limited* (1979) and the *Bremer Vulkan* case previously mentioned. These cases confirm the power of the court to grant an injunction restraining claimants in an arbitration from proceeding when thay have been guilty of inordinate delay in pursuing the matter – particularly, when a fair hearing is thereby prejudiced. Now, under SS.5(1) and (2) of the 1979 Act, the court may, upon application, make an order permitting an arbitrator or umpire to proceed on an *'ex parte'* basis in such circumstances – with the corollary of empowering him to close the proceedings by issuing an award which, in effect, dismisses the claim for want of prosecution and apportions the liability for the related costs accordingly.

In Scotland

In Scotland, the terms 'arbiter' and 'oversman' are used respectively in place of the terms 'arbitrator' and 'umpire' in England and Wales. Scottish arbitration proceedings have their basis in the Law as developed in Scotland and differ from English practice in that the Statutes which regulate such proceedings apply only to

(a) the 'reduction' of an award where the arbiter has conducted himself contrary to the laws of Natural Justice and has issued an award under the influence of 'corruption, bribery or falsehood' (S.25: Articles of Regulation 1695);

(b) the appointment of 'any one Arbiter, 3, 5 or 7 Arbiters by the lawful direction of the court or the Lord Ordinary to sit as a jury' (S.50: Court of Session (Scotland) Act 1850);

(c) (i) the appointment of an un-named holder of office (e.g. president of a named Body);
(ii) the appointment of an arbiter by the court where there is no provision in the contract and the parties fail to agree;
(iii) the appointment of an arbiter where the contract provides for the election of two arbiters and one party fails to elect;
(iv) the conference of power to the court to appoint an oversman where either the contract omits power to the two arbiters or the contract is

silent on the appointment of an oversman;
(v) governing the procedure by petition to a Lord Ordinary or a sheriff. (Arbitration (Scotland) Act 1894);

(d) provision for Summary Trial by a particular Lord Ordinary (Court of Session) acting as Arbiter;
(The Administration of Justice (Scotland) Act 1933);

(e) the power of an Arbiter to state a case on law to the Court of Session on the application of one of the parties. This provision can be contracted out in contracts drawn up 'post' the enactment;
(The Administration of Justice (Scotland) Act 1972); and

(f) statutory Arbitrations are regulated by legislation which is complementary to the position in England and Wales, e.g. the Lands Clauses Consolidation (Scotland) Act 1845, the Hill Farming (Scotland) Act 1946, Agricultural Holdings Acts etc.

The administration of arbitration proceedings in Scotland is usually dealt with by a Clerk (normally a Solicitor) appointed by the Arbiter. The Clerk acts as advisor to the arbiter on matters of law and procedure, the direction of Interlocutors and the preparation of the Record prior to any hearing. Colloquially, the Clerk's function is known as 'the post box' – to keep the arbiter from direct contact with the parties or their agents during the interlocutory stages.

Procedure for the enforcement of foreign awards in Scotland is complementary to that under English law. S.41 of the Arbitration Act 1950 provides that Part II of that Act applies to Scotland subject to certain amendments. Otherwise, the 'English' arbitration acts do not apply to Scotland.

Historically, reference may also be made to the *Regiam Majestatem* (said to have originated in about the twelfth century) where reference is made to the regulation of arbitration hearings, the appointment of arbiters, the death of the arbiter, etc. This is a Scottish legal treatise by an unknown author and so-called from its opening words. Its four volumes include a collection of handy reference material compiled from Roman law and other early legal codes and statutes.

In Northern Ireland

For Northern Ireland the relative legislation is embodied in The Arbitration Act (Northern Ireland) 1937 as amended by the Northern Ireland Act 1962. This follows closely the provisions of Part I of the 1950 Act which, by S.34 (as amended by the 1975 Act), excludes any application of that Part of the 1950 Act to Northern Ireland, while S.42 thereof stipulates that Part II of the 1950 Act (amended as detailed) is applicable. The 1975 Act extends to Northern Ireland but the 1979 Act does not.

In the Channel Islands

In the Channel Islands the parties and their chosen arbitrator enter into an *ad hoc* tri-partite agreement which, *inter alia,* sets out the matter/s in dispute, the procedure to be followed in the arbitration proceedings – in particular, the means for clarifying any point of law – and, usually, providing an indemnity for the arbitrator against any charge of negligence. Such agreements are registered and supervised by the States authorities.

In the Isle of Man

The Isle of Man has its own Arbitration Acts. The 1975 Act replaced their Arbitration Acts 1910–35, based on the 1950 and the 1975 Acts of England and Wales. The latest relevant enactment is the Arbitration (International Investment Disputes) Act 1983.

In the Republic of Ireland (Eire)

The Arbitration Act 1954 became effective on 1 January 1955. It provides for four general categories of arbitration:

1 voluntary;
2 statutory;
3 arbitrations arising out of references by the High Court;
4 foreign Arbitral awards.

The third category provides for the court to refer questions of fact to arbitration. This, presumably, is a convenient procedure when, for example, the parties are disputing matters of a technical/professional nature which the judge may feel himself to be less qualified to decide than a suitably experienced practitioner. The arbitrator so appointed can be asked to adjudicate on technical arguments and report back – an interesting two-way interrelationship between arbitration and court proceedings.

The 1954 Act has three schedules:

I Protocol on Arbitration Clauses: Geneva: opened on 24 September 1923.
II Convention on Execution of Foreign Arbitral Awards: Geneva: 26 September 1927.
III Repeals *(inter alia)* – An Act for Determining Differences by Arbitration: 10 Will. 3c.14(Ir).

Incidentally, the text of the 1927 Geneva Convention is set out as the Second Schedule of the 1950 Act (England and Wales). Eire has not yet adopted the 1958 New York Convention.

In Other Countries

Other countries have also legislated with reference to arbitration. They include the majority of past and present members of the British Commonwealth as well as France, West Germany, Netherlands, United States, Japan, Belgium, Norway, Sweden, Spain. All such countries recognise the need to reinforce their arbitration procedures by varying degrees of legislation.

International Disputes

From what has been stated about the general application of arbitration to the settlement of commercial disputes, it will be no surprise to discover that arbitration also has its place in international affairs. In the field of inter-state *litigation* the supreme court is the International Court of Justice at The Hague. Inter-State arbitration is the subject of the 1907 Hague Convention which includes the statement: 'International Arbitration has for its object the settlement of disputes between States by judges of their own choice on the basis of respect for law.' These principles have been maintained despite the many successive changes in international groupings and working relationships under such bodies as the League of Nations and, later, the United Nations. It remains to be seen what further developments take place under the Treaty of Rome (EEC) and other 'Blocs'.

In addition, a considerable amount of arbitration takes place in international commercial disputes but this highly complex field is likely to be outside the normal competence/experience of the non-legal practitioner. Those concerned will find a useful collection of the Rules etc., promulgated by various bodies in Schmitthoff's *International Commercial Arbitration.*

2 Arbitration v. Litigation

Litigation (Civil)

As most people are aware, litigation is the process whereby disputes are settled by submitting them to the decision of one or more judges in a court of law. The ascending order of judicial competence of the civil courts in England, Wales and Northern Ireland is: the County Court (CC), the High Court (HC), the Court of Appeal (CA) and the House of Lords (HL). Since the UK joined the EEC, final decisions in certain cases are governed by Community Law – as administered, for example, by the Court of Human Rights at Strasbourg.

The civil courts under the Scottish legal system have different names and functions but, as for the rest of the UK, the supreme court is the House of Lords – subject, again, to the operation of Community Law.

Arbitration (Commercial)

The nature and role of arbitration in the settlement of disputes is not properly understood by some and it is necessary to explain what the term may or may not embrace. Depending upon the basis on which it is set up, arbitration may be

(a) a voluntary judicial process to ascertain, declare and enforce the respective rights and obligations of the parties; or,
(b) a statutory judicial process within the scope and functions of relevant legislation; or,
(c) a non-judicial process to ascertain and declare (but not to enforce) what, in the opinion of the competent board, tribunal, arbitrator or umpire, the respective rights and obligations of the parties ought to be – for example, in trade disputes.

Arbitration is not

(a) conciliation; or,

(b) an agreement between the parties to be bound by (1) counsel's opinion, or (2) a valuer's appraisal or valuation, or (3) principles of natural justice; or,
(c) adjudication under certain provisions of standard forms of contract or sub-contract used in the construction industry; or
(d) the issue of a certificate by the architect, supervising officer or engineer under the contract for the execution of construction works; or,
(e) the reference of questions arising out of sporting contests to the appropriate officials of the sport in question.

Unless otherwise indicated, the term 'arbitration' as used in this book means 'commercial arbitration': that is to say, a process whereby disputes arising on commercial contracts are settled by arbitration under the provisions of the Arbitration Acts 1950–79. This, in effect, comes within the limited meaning of 'a voluntary judicial process to ascertain, declare and enforce the respective rights and obligations of the parties' to a commercial contract mentioned above. However, even that limited meaning has profound implications.

Time and Cost

Parties contemplating legal proceedings will want to know what they are risking in terms of cost before committing themselves to such a course either by litigation or arbitration. Unfortunately, it is seldom possible for their advisors to provide anything like a firm estimate; *'It all depends . . .'* they will say. In practice, cost is directly related to the time expended upon or in connection with the matter by everyone involved – legal advisors (solicitors and, perhaps, counsel), witnesses (both 'general' and 'expert') and the parties themselves. Those factors, at least, are common to both litigation and arbitration proceedings. Furthermore, in arbitration the fees and expenses of the arbitrator/s have to be met – although, it is argued, those charges can be 'saved', in some cases, by a substantial reduction in the total time required for the hearing of the case compared with court proceedings. The suggestion that some arbitration cases take as long and cost as much as they would if taken through the court may be related to the (sometimes) over-involvement of lawyers and the corresponding parallelism with court procedure. Thus, it can be seen, the main factor – time – is very largely governed by the way in which the parties decide to proceed and how they choose to conduct their side of the proceedings.

Not surprisingly, there is a perennial argument whether arbitration or litigation is the better way to proceed in the settlement of disputes. Some claim that arbitration is relatively quicker and, therefore, cheaper than litigation but others do not agree. Whatever the merits of such arguments, arbitration is neither quick nor cheap in real terms and everyone involved in arbitration proceedings should devote their best efforts to persuading the parties to settle their dispute at the earliest possible date – having regard to all the circumstances – but some disputants, having set themselves on a particular course, may be difficult to deflect. In the space of a few months a builder was the claimant in two cases before different arbitrators. The claims were almost identical; the builder was concerned in both but they involved different clients and their respective architects. When the builder heard that he had won the first case his advocate strongly recommended the respondent's advocate in the second case to advise his client to settle. The client would not agree and when the award in the second case was published it was almost a carbon copy of the first one. It cannot be over-emphasised that the purpose of arbitration proceedings is to arrive at a settlement. The corollary is that such settlement can and should be encouraged at all stages so that, if possible, the parties can avoid or, at least, mitigate the time, cost and stress expended in going right through to the bitter end.

Privacy/Intimacy of Proceedings

Among other advantages claimed for arbitration is the fact that the proceedings are private; also, that it is less complicated and formal than Court procedure. From some points of view that is a pity because, in consequence, there is no such thing as Case Law arising out of arbitration as such. The decision of one arbitrator cannot be pleaded in another case – for the simple reason that each case is dealt with on its merits, with the minimum formality, and the award is not made public. Furthermore, subject to the limited provisions of the 1979 Act, awards under normal UK procedure do not state reasons for the decisions given therein and this is another practical obstacle to the subsequent pleading of previous decisions even if awards, as such, were to become public knowledge.

Arbitrator's Expertise

Another advantage claimed for arbitration is that an arbitrator is often able to bring his own knowledge and experience to bear on the proceedings; he does not need to be told about professional practice, trade customs or what is meant by technical terms. On the other hand, a judge may have to have such things explained in great detail. And, it should be remembered, an essential feature of English arbitration proceedings is the right of access to the High Court for general guidance and rulings on questions of law – albeit restricted by the 1979 Act. The arbitrator, having experience and knowledge of the background to the matters in dispute becomes, in effect, a 'third expert'. This, it has been suggested, is or could be undesirable; others argue that this is the whole point of having an expert as the arbitrator and is one of the most attractive features of the arbitration process.

Other Considerations

It has also been contended that arbitration ought not to be prescribed in any contract as the only way of settling future disputes. This is because, when any such dispute does in fact arise, it could then be seen to be better for the parties to go direct to the court. It can also be claimed that a judge, being a professional lawyer, is better able to decide between conflicting evidence when an expert called by one party is contradicted by someone equally eminent called by the other side. But, again, that contention can be countered by referring to an arbitrator's expertise.

A further consideration of relevance in some cases is that 'legal aid' under the provisions of the Legal Aid and Advice Act 1949, and subsequent enactments, is not available to any party in arbitration proceedings – whatever his financial position may be. Therefore, if a party would qualify for such assistance in court proceedings, it is arguably unfair to prevent his doing so by enforcing an agreement to refer future disputes to arbitration.

Another objection to arbitration is based on the fact that questions of law or disputes about awards can only be settled finally by the court and, in doing so, the court seldom (if ever) reopens questions of fact since the arbitrator is deemed to have heard all the evidence and to have come to a proper view about such matters. On the other hand, if the dispute had been tried in open court, all relevant facts would become known to the court before any decision about them was made.

Because of this sort of debate it can be seen why some views are weighted in favour of making it optional instead of mandatory to refer disputes to arbitration under the provisions of standard forms of contract and standard conditions of trading. In 1957, for example, the Metropolitan Boroughs Standing Joint Committee considered a recommendation from the General Purposes Committee of Westminster City Council, supporting the contention of what was then the Chelsea Borough Council, that building contracts should not provide in advance for the compulsory reference of disputes to arbitration – leaving it open for the parties to do so if they so wished. More recently, during the House of Lords debates on the Unfair Contract Terms Bill, the Lord Chancellor (Lord Elwyn Jones) moved a new clause providing, in effect, that a consumer could opt out from the provisions of an arbitration clause in a consumer trading transaction. That clause was duly approved but eventually negatived upon the bill returning to the House of Commons.

Possible Reforms

It is clear that arbitration, like many another human institution, may not be perfect but works reasonably well despite the delaying tactics which are sometimes adopted by a reluctant party. When alternative methods of procedure are examined it is not easy to be convinced that they would produce any better results than are achieved under existing arrangements.

Among various potential innovations which have been mooted, a suggestion was made some years ago that there ought to be a permanent court of arbitration, where people could go to get their disputes settled, presided over by a lawyer with a professional assessor to help him in professional/technical matters. To some extent, this service is now available in the County Courts. It has been argued also that much time and expense would be saved if there were an understanding that no lawyers would be present at arbitration Hearings. That is to say, the proceedings before the arbitrator would not be conducted by lawyers but, of course, the parties would be free to consult them about the merits of their case and the way it should be presented. However, in the course of delivering the 1977 Alexander Lecture to the Institute of Arbitrators, Lord Justice Roskill warned against excluding legal representation. He said: 'I have always thought that those trade associations who exclude legal representation under their arbitration rules make a grave mistake in denying themselves of help, as has been manifested time and again by the unhappy state in which some of their special cases come before the courts.'

Speaking at the 1954 Conference of the Institute of Arbitrators in Cambridge, Mr Norman Royce supported a suggestion made over ten years previously by Mr J. R. W. Alexander. He said:

> I believe that there could be some merit in holding a hearing in two stages. At the first stage the parties could be heard by an arbitrator, who conducts the proceedings in a reasonably informal manner, and deduces the issues from hearing the facts. The parties would have the opportunity, if they both agreed, to have the case decided at that stage and for the arbitrator to publish his award – with a time limit fixed for those proceedings. If, however, the parties decide against the decision being given at that stage, they would have the opportunity of requiring the (first) arbitrator to submit a report as to the facts to the second stage, where the case would be heard by another arbitrator in the manner applicable to the usual arbitration procedure, with counsel appearing.

Mr Royce went on to imply that when facts only are the subject of the (first) arbitrator's findings he would support such findings with 'reasons' – presumably, in the way he would if appointed in connection with an action in the County Court when, having been supplied with the arbitrator's findings of facts and the reasons for so finding, the judge takes the case to a conclusion.

It is interesting to see, nearly thirty years later, that the dispute–settlement procedure prescribed in the ACA Form of Building Agreement 1982 follows the Royce/Alexander suggestion mentioned above by importing a first-stage 'adjudication'. But, in doing so, the ACA has departed from the implied stipulation by Royce that the adjudicator should not become the arbitrator in the same dispute.

The foregoing comments/suggestions are mentioned here to highlight the flexibility which is available to parties when they are considering the drafting of an arbitration agreement. Every existing institution and its procedures must be open to the question whether what is being done could be done better by a different process and/or by different people.

This sort of monitoring is essential because the natural progression for everything is to deteriorate and, now and again, most things need reassessment and a new injection of thought or action in the light of changing circumstances. Arbitration procedures are as likely as anything else to require up-dating to meet changing contemporary needs and it is in that context that the Arbitration Act 1979 was enacted.

Moves Towards the 1979 Act

It had become increasingly evident that note would have to be taken of the criticism directed by our E.E.C. colleagues and other foreign interests against certain features of the English arbitration system; that is to say

1 the fact that awards were not required to state the reasons on which the findings were based;
2 the case-stated (or 'special case') procedure whereby delay could be caused, sometimes vexatiously, by a party;
3 the inability of parties to contract out of their right of appeal because, it was held, to do so would be an improper attempt to oust the jurisdiction of the court.

These were said to be the main reasons why foreign parties were reluctant to submit to arbitration in London and, consequently, to English law and, as such, were mentioned in the debate in the House of Lords on 15 May 1978. In replying to that debate, the Lord Chancellor (Lord Elwyn Jones) indicated his willingness to consider the general question of amending the Arbitration Act provisions in so far as they apply to cases with a foreign element and, accordingly, he introduced the Arbitration Bill in the House of Lords on 28 November 1978. This, in due course, led to the passing of the Arbitration Act 1979 which, *inter alia,* removed certain objections to traditional English practice.

3 How Arbitration Arises

Arbitration Agreements

While anyone may be taken to court, no one can be made to enter upon arbitration proceedings unless he has agreed to do so.

Without weakening the emphasis on the principle that, for practical purposes, arbitration agreements should be in writing, it has to be said that it is valid to make such an agreement orally – which can be operated quite successfully as long as all parties continue to honour it. Of course, problems which may arise thereon cannot be dealt with under the Arbitration Acts, and the only recourse then open to an aggrieved party is to the court under his common law rights. This, for obvious reasons, is likely to be a 'difficult row to hoe'.

The minimum requirement to constitute a valid and enforceable arbitration agreement is succinctly defined in S.32 of the Arbitration Act 1950 as: 'a written agreement to submit present or future differences to arbitration whether an arbitrator is named therein or not'. This is confirmed, and to some extent amplified, by S.7(1) of the 1975 Act and S.7(1)(e) of the 1979 Act. However, to be fully effective, an arbitration agreement should also specify the matters which are thus referrable and any other provisions which the Parties may wish to incorporate about procedure and other matters within the discretion allowed to them by the 1950 Act.

The 1950 Act allows the parties to agree and express their wishes with regard to particular features of the arbitration process by which any dispute between them shall be resolved. This is evident by the recurring phrase: 'Unless a contrary intention is expressed . . .' That is to say, in the relevant arbitration agreement. Accordingly, in drawing-up any such agreement, parties are free to amend what is otherwise binding upon them by making stipulations about some or all of the following matters

(a) the revocation of the arbitrator's authority (S.1);
(b) the composition of the tribunal (S.6);
(c) the appointment of an umpire when an arbitrator is appointed by each party (S.8(1));

(d) the functions of an umpire when two arbitrators fail to agree (S.8(2));
(e) the examination of the parties by the arbitrator (or umpire) on oath or affirmation or at all (S.12(1));
(f) the production of documents to the arbitrator (or umpire) and compliance with any other requirements of the arbitrator (or umpire) (S.12(1));
(g) the examination of witnesses under oath or affirmation (S.12(3));
(h) the making of interim awards (S.14);
(i) the ordering of specific performance (S.15);
(j) the finality of the award to be made by the arbitrator (or umpire) (S.16);
(k) the correction of 'slips' in the award (S.17);
(l) the arbitrator's discretion with regard to the apportionment of liability; for costs of the reference between the parties and his power to tax and settle such costs (S.18(1)).

Furthermore, within their general freedom to enter into whatever legal agreements they wish, the parties can include stipulations about such matters as: the maximum number of expert witnesses to be called by each side, their agreement that the matters in dispute be referred and adjudged on the basis of written submissions and related documents only, the date and the place of the hearing, the matters referrable to arbitration, when any such matters may or may not be referred, the sort of person to be (or not to be) the arbitrator. Reference is made in Chapter 1 to the fact that 'exclusion agreements' related to domestic arbitration can be made only after a dispute has arisen. Therefore, when drafting the terms of any *post-dispute* arbitration agreement it is possible, if so required, to incorporate the exclusion provisions previously mentioned. In connection with international trading agreements it is also prudent to specify the law, the language and the locale for any related proceedings.

In many trading relationships, an 'arbitration agreement' exists as a clause in the conditions of contract which govern such relationships. It is not necessary for such an agreement to be expressed in any particular manner – it can be contained, for example, in an exchange of letters between the parties. Thus, provided the essentials are incorporated, the basic conditions are satisfied. In other circumstances, the parties may wish to have an *ad hoc* arbitration agreement drawn up by their respective legal advisors.

It is important to distinguish between an 'umbrella' agreement to refer *future* disputes to arbitration and the submission of a *current* dispute to a particular arbitrator. It follows that there must be an identifiable dispute or difference between the parties before they can proceed to arbitration but, in practice, it sometimes happens that the parties need help in identifying what their differences really are – especially in the context of an agglomerate of facts (or alleged facts), claims and counter-claims and other features of a complex situation.

Death of a Party or Arbitrator

S.2 of the 1950 Act provides that the death of a party to an arbitration agreement does not affect its validity and that it is thereupon enforceable by or against his personal representative/s. Correspondingly, the authority of an arbitrator is not affected by the death of any party to the agreement under which he is appointed.

When the appointed arbitrator dies or refuses to act or becomes incapable of acting in the matter, the parties (or either of them) can apply to the court under S.10 of the 1950 Act with the object of having a new arbitrator appointed. When that has been achieved the proceedings revert to the proverbial 'square one' except to the extent that the new arbitrator agrees (or is required by the parties) to confirm and/or adopt what has gone before. The parties are inevitably at risk in respect of any extra cost which could be incurred in consequence of any such new appointment and, in cases when the proceedings are likely to be protracted, parties may be advised to consider the desirability of insuring against such risk by effecting an insurance policy related to the life-expectation of the arbitrator.

Delays

Delay due to disagreement about whether the parties to an arbitration agreement intended any future dispute between them to be referred to one or more arbitrators is avoided by S.6 of the 1950 Act which states that, unless it is otherwise specifically stipulated, every such agreement is deemed to provide that future disputes thereunder be referred to a single arbitrator.

It is also stipulated by the 1950 Act (S.8) that when in any such agreement it is provided that, when a dispute arises, one arbitrator is to be appointed by each party, those arbitrators must themselves appoint an umpire. The time when such umpire is to be appointed is clarified by S.6 of the 1979 Act as being at any time but, in any case, immediately upon the two arbitrators failing to agree.

The umpire plays no active part in the proceedings unless the two arbitrators fail to agree or the court so orders – whereupon he proceeds as would a sole arbitrator and the original arbitrators assume the role of advocates before him. This arrangement is common in international commercial disputes and is the usual one in arbitration proceedings related to maritime disputes.

Another possibility envisaged by the 1950 Act is that the arbitration tribunal is composed of three arbitrators in accordance with the provisions of a particular agreement. Although S.9 was amended by S.6(2) of the 1979 Act, it still provides that an award agreed by a majority of arbitrators is binding. The same principle is applicable to any (odd) number of arbitrators.

4 Appointment of Arbitrator

Who Can Be an Arbitrator?

An arbitrator is any person who has jurisdiction, either alone or as a member of a board or tribunal, to hear and determine a dispute referred to arbitration. In Scotland, the term 'arbiter' is used – a more direct derivative of the Latin *arbiter* meaning 'one who goes to see'. Thus, anyone who is not incompetent by reason of mental disability or other valid disqualification is able to act as arbitrator if he/she has been properly nominated and, being willing so to act, has accepted the appointment. It is prudent for parties to make the widest possible enquiries as to the suitability and availability of persons who could be appointed. It is useless to complain at a later stage that a particular appointment was unfortunate – or worse. Persons nominated by an appointing third party, on the other hand, will be known to be not only competent but also available in advance of any such nomination.

So, how does a particular person become the arbitrator in a particular case? In the majority of cases he will be in that role because the parties have so agreed or, if the parties have been unable to do so, because he has been appointed (or nominated) by a third party to whom the parties have agreed to entrust such appointment (or nomination). There are several good reasons why the parties should, if possible, agree upon the person to be appointed as arbitrator rather than leaving him to be nominated by a third-party. These include the saving of time and, possibly, costs. However, there is often a natural reluctance by one party to agree a single nominee put forward by the initiating party and it is better, therefore, to put forward the names of three or four persons from whom the other party may select the one he prefers or, at any rate, has least objection to.

Official Referees

Under the Administration of Justice Act 1956, cases which involve a considerable amount of detailed investigation into, for example, measurements, costings and other data, could be referred to an 'Official Referee', one of several experienced barristers of not less than ten years standing retained by the court for that purpose. Now, since the repeal of that Act by S.25 of the Courts Act 1975, the erstwhile functions of Official Referees are performed by judge-arbitrators – as explained below. Thus, while the term 'official referee' may still be used it is, in fact, obsolete but the term 'official referee's business' is retained.

Judge-arbitrators: Judge-umpires

It is possible for certain judges to act as arbitrators (or umpires) – such roles being referred to as 'judge-arbitrator' (or 'judge-umpire'). These are circuit judges of the Commercial Court in the Queens Bench Division of the High Court appointed by the Lord Chancellor for that purpose and who, if available, accept appointment as sole arbitrator or umpire under an arbitration agreement as empowered by S.4(1) of the Administration of Justice Act 1970; their status and functions are defined in Schedule 3 of that Act. S.5 of the 1979 Act empowers a judge-arbitrator/umpire to make any order which, as a judge, he could make in respect of an application under any arbitration proceedings. A further advantage, as some would claim, of having a HC judge as arbitrator (or umpire) is that any appeal arising on his award can (subject to the provisions of the 1979 Act) go direct to the CA. Other judges and officials of the HC may also act as arbitrators in their private capacities but, in so acting, have the same status as any other arbitrator irrespective of their status in the court. Judges and Registrars of County Courts can act as arbitrators but derive their powers to do so from S.92 of the County Courts Act 1959 as such proceedings are excluded from the provisions of the Arbitration Acts 1950 and 1979.

Appointing (or Nominating) Authorities

At this point some clarification of an 'appointing' third-party's function may be appropriate; does he *appoint* or does he merely *nominate* the (potential) arbitrator? It is better, in practice, to think in terms whereby the arbitrator is *nominated* in such circumstances because, before he can properly take jurisdiction, he must formally accept the appointment – subject, it may be, to any stipulations he makes with regard to his fees or other matters. So, there are two essential steps leading to the arbitrator's appointment – nomination and acceptance; that is to say: *Nomination + Acceptance = Appointment.* Thereafter the arbitrator is seated firmly in the chair, so to speak, and cannot be removed except by an order of the court.

An 'appointing' third-party is often specified in arbitration agreements – in particular, those which are expressed as a clause in the conditions of a contract. For example, under the JCT Standard Form of Building Contract that function is allotted to the President of the Royal Institute of British Architects (RIBA) and under the JCT Standard Form of Sub-Contract (NSC/4) it is given to the President of the Royal Institution of Chartered Surveyors (RICS) unless the applicant opts for an appointment by the President, RIBA. When there is no such provision (and even when there is) such 'third-party' can be the subject of (further) agreement between the parties.

It is not unknown for delay to be caused by the failure of an appointing third-party to nominate an arbitrator in accordance with the terms of an arbitration agreement – to which, it must be remembered, the appointing authority is not a party. Now, under S.6(4) of the 1979 Act, any such delay can be the subject of Notice by a party and, if the failure to nominate then continues for more than seven days, an application can be made to the court for the necessary appointment.

Another sort of third-party appointment is by the court under S.10 of the 1950 Act.

Security for Arbitrator's Fees/Expenses

A question which often arises when a potential arbitrator is deciding whether to accept a particular appointment is whether, in due course, he will obtain payment of his fees and expenses without undue difficulty. If he deems it necessary, the potential arbitrator can stipulate, as one of the conditions under which he is prepared to accept the appointment, that a specified sum be deposited – either by one of the parties or by each of them jointly – as security for his fees etc. Although it is not obligatory to do so, such sum should be placed with a trustee/stake-holder with the proviso that it shall be released as and when stipulated by the arbitrator or, in the event of his death or incapacity, by an order of the court. It could be further provided that any interest accruing to such sum be retained by the stake-holder in consideration of his services.

Immunity of Arbitrators

Another vitally important question for arbitrators is whether they can be sued for alleged negligence in their conduct of arbitration proceedings. The long-standing presumption that arbitrators, like judges, are immune from such liability was put in doubt by some comments by Lord Kilbrandon in his judgment when *Arenson* v. *Casson Beckman Rutley and Company* (1975) came before the House of Lords. His Lordship leaned towards the view that arbitrators, like valuers, owe a duty to the parties who appoint them and, consequently, are equally liable to those parties in respect of any negligence. He went on to suggest that if this were the generally accepted view it would become common practice for arbitration agreements to provide immunity for arbitrators by including an undertaking whereby the parties agree not to sue the arbitrator in respect of any liability he might otherwise incur in connection with any related arbitration proceedings. However, Lord Kilbrandon's comments referred to above were not relevant to the main issue and, as such, may not have binding effect. Furthermore, arbitrators can take comfort from Lord Denning's remarks in the course of his judgment in the Court of Appeal in *Campbell* v. *Edwards* (1976) when, after considering the House of Lords decision in the *Arenson* case, he said:

> The position of a valuer is very different from an arbitrator. If a valuer is negligent in making a valuation he may be sued by the party – vendor or purchaser – who is injured by his wrong valuation. But an arbitrator is different. In my opinion he cannot be sued by either party to the dispute, even if he is negligent. The only remedy of the party is to set aside the award, and then only if it comes within the accepted grounds for setting aside. If an arbitrator is guilty of misconduct, his award can be set aside. If he has gone wrong on a point of law, which appears on the face of it, it can be corrected by the court. But the arbitrator himself is not liable to be sued. I say this because I should be sorry if any doubt should be felt about it.

The main point of all that seems to be that arbitrators must not only be *said* to be acting as such but also be *seen* to be so acting in order to enjoy the immunity referred to by Lord Denning. Whatever title he takes or is given, the person who merely performs the function of valuer, certifier or *quasi-arbitrator* does not enjoy such immunity and may be liable, therefore, for the consequences of any negligence in the performance of his duties.

Nevertheless, some doubt may still remain about the position of arbitrators who, having failed to agree in a two-arbitrator-plus-umpire reference, become the advocates of their respective 'appointers' in presenting the case to the umpire. It may be prudent for such arbitrators to protect themselves by the sort of indemnity referred to above in connection with Lord Kilbrandon's comments in the *Arenson* case but, in the light of court decisions in *Rondel* v. *Worsley* (1969) and *Saif Ali and An'or* v. *Sydney Mitchell and Co.* (1978), such additional protection would seem to be unnecessary.

Statutory Appointments

Another way by which an arbitrator may arrive on a particular scene is by a statutory appointment. It has been previously mentioned that under various Statutes it is provided that disputes about certain matters be referred to arbitration and, in some cases, such enactments prescribe in what circumstances and by whom the arbitrator is to be appointed; alternatively, it may be provided that the particular question shall be referred to a judge-arbitrator or to a tribunal which, again, may be a standing or an *ad hoc* body.

Arbitrator's Jurisdiction

It is important for any arbitrator to ensure that the formal establishment of his own status and role is clear and unchallengeable; until this is so it is pointless to try to initiate the proceedings. It could be like a spectator at a football match attempting to control the game by blowing a whistle to which nobody pays any attention. Therefore, before he finally agrees to act, the arbitrator should satisfy himself that he is competent to do so – professionally and jurisdictionally. He must not allow himself to be so dazzled by the prospect of sitting as a 'judge' that he fails to ask himself the question: 'Well, is it something that I ought to be doing anyway?' Upon reflection he may feel it is a matter in which he would prefer not to be involved; or it may be a case where, for one reason or another, he feels himself to be incompetent or disqualified. He may, for instance, have some personal connection with one of the parties or he may be known for his strong views on a particular issue. If so, and in any case of doubt, the 'invited arbitrator' should firmly decline to become involved. In other circumstances he may doubt whether he has or could be given jurisdiction; is the dispute, for example, a matter which can be dealt with by arbitration in the way the parties have stipulated?

Or, is one of the parties under a building contract, for example, raising a matter which cannot be dealt with until the work has been completed? Obviously, any attempt by one party to get arbitration proceedings moving in the absence of proper clearance could be promptly blocked by the other party.

So, for all sorts of reasons, the arbitrator (or arbitrator-designate) is wise to pause and weigh up the whole situation and not to rush into things too precipitously. It is imprudent of him to act until the arrangements are properly parcelled-up and all loose ends tied in a properly established arbitration package.

Arbitrator's Impartiality and Efficiency

From the moment he is appointed, the arbitrator should be very careful not to be – or appear to be – in touch with either party in the absence of the other at any time. On one occasion, two men met over a pre-lunch drink and, after talking for a while, exchanged names. One said: 'That's interesting; I think you have been appointed arbitrator in a case in which I am acting for a client'. 'Well,' said the other, 'in that case I should not be talking to you', and he walked away. It is as real as that for, however discreet and trustworthy any such persons are, the fact that they were seen to be in conversation (about a voyage to the moon or anything else) could be thought suspicious and must, therefore, be avoided.

Reference is made elsewhere to the possibility that one of the parties may be reluctant to proceed, but what can the parties, or either of them, do to expedite matters when the arbitrator himself fails to keep things moving? If all other means of persuasion have been unsuccessful the party concerned can apply to the Court for the appropriate order – either directing the arbitrator to get things moving or, in extreme circumstances, removing him for want of diligence or other disqualifying factors. Such factors include the display of bias and having an interest in the matter/s referred – as exemplified by court decisions in two cases brought against licensing Justices – *R.* v. *Sheffield Confirming Authority, ex parte Truswell's Brewery Company Limited* (1937) and *R.* v. *Barnsley County Borough Licensing Justices, ex parte Barnsley and District Licensed Victuallers Association* (1960).

It follows that any such disqualifying factor could be the ground on which the court can be asked to remove an arbitrator or umpire and appoint another in his place.

What is written above about the appointment, status and functions of an arbitrator, is related, particularly, to the role of a *sole* arbitrator but, subject to some obvious differences between their respective roles and functions, the foregoing comments about sole arbitrators are also applicable in general to the combination of two or more arbitrators and to umpires.

Land and Property

Disputes arising from the valuation of land or any interest in land to which statutory authorities are parties are referrable to the Lands Tribunal under the Lands Tribunal Act 1949. However, it should be mentioned that in many sorts of contract including leases and other agreements related to the tenure of land and/or property, it is provided that disputes arising thereon shall be settled by arbitration. Questions in respect of rent reviews, for example, are often the subject of references to arbitration in accordance with the procedure stipulated in the relevant provisions of such documents.

5 Interlocutory Proceedings

Preparation of Claim

Parties in dispute do not go to arbitration without a good deal of preliminary activity at various stages. Arbitration proceedings do not erupt suddenly; they are the latest stage reached in a protracted series of meetings, telephone calls, letters, arguments and as many other displays of human behaviour as can be imagined. Even so, when parties reach the point of deadlock and an arbitration is being thought of seriously, the question arises how to prepare for it. The main preliminary matter is for the claimant to prepare his claim in the arbitration proceedings. This, usually, will be a matter of re-presenting the facts and figures (or some of them) which have been bandied around for some time. However, one of the first tasks of the arbitrator in a particular case may be to ensure that the parties have agreed what it is they are in dispute about. If they have not, he should help them to define their differences in specific terms. Another common problem is to decide which party is, effectively, the claimant. Normally, he is the one who initiates the proceedings but, if it transpires that the other party (the initial respondent) has the greater claim, the arbitrator may order that the respective roles are reversed.

It may be helpful, at this stage, to distinguish between the terms 'Statement of Claim' and 'Points of Claim'. The former is a fully detailed statement of what is being claimed and the reasons why it is suggested such claims should be met – with all supporting documents attached or otherwise incorporated. This is of value to the claimant for its own sake and/or for briefing his advocate in arbitration proceedings. Alternatively, it can be used as the submission made by a claimant when a dispute has been referred to arbitration on the basis of written submissions and documentary evidence only. On the other hand, a document entitled 'Points of Claim' is intended to be only a summarised statement setting out the heads of claim, the amount/s claimed and a general indication of the supporting evidence it is intended to bring before the arbitrator at the hearing – so that the other side is not then taken by surprise.

There is no prescribed form in which a claim should be prepared and presented; this allows scope for personal capacity and ingenuity in presentation but, needless to say, it ought to be clear, concise and factual; it should concentrate on those things which are relevant and avoid other things which are not. It may be better for someone who has not been involved in the preliminary bickering to prepare the case for arbitration because most people cannot help becoming emotionally involved in something with which they have been personally concerned. Whether the whole thing is handed over to somebody else or not, the point is that a fresh mind can often help to pick out those things which are really important as distinct from those that are only incidental to the main issue. Eventually, after much head-scratching perhaps, the claim, together with all relevant documents such as letters, minutes of meetings, photographs, drawings, schedules, samples, reports and anything else that has a bearing should be put together in as neat and concise a manner as possible.

Scott Schedule

A convenient method of presenting to the arbitrator a summary of the respective contentions and evaluations submitted by the parties in their respective Points of Claim and Points of Counter-Claim, if any, is by means of a 'Scott Schedule' – sometimes referred to as an 'Official Referee's Schedule'. This is a multi-column précis of the points of claim against which the submissions by the respective parties are shown in separate columns, with the provision of a further (blank) column in which the arbitrator can in due course enter his own findings. A typical form of presenting a Scott Schedule is shown in (7), Part III. These are minimum requirements but any particular schedule can have as many other columns as may be necessary.

The 'mechanics' of preparing a Scott Schedule will be either as agreed by the parties or in accordance with an order by the arbitrator, if necessary. Subject to any such agreement or order, it is reasonable to expect that a Scott Schedule would be initiated by the claimant then, as a second stage development, added to by the respondent. The third stage is completed when the claimant has added his replies to the points made by the respondent and the schedule is then ready for submission to the arbitrator (or judge-arbitrator) as and when required.

Any figures (i.e., quantities, prices, amounts) mentioned in the pleadings should be as far as possible agreed (as figures) between the parties before the hearing – even though any liability or other implication thereof remains in dispute. In this respect, also, the Scott Schedule will reveal at a glance where figures are in fact agreed and, where not agreed, the sort of gap between them.

The preparation and presentation of their case by each side will be referred to again but at this point a digression is necessary to consider the legal and professional/technical advice and assistance which the parties may be wise to enlist in all but the simplest sorts of dispute.

Legal Advice/Assistance

A layman who is not experienced in such matters and who finds himself in a dispute will be well advised to consult a solicitor. This is as far as he may need to go but, in some circumstances, the solicitor may advise him to seek Counsel's opinion and, having done so, it could then be decided to settle the matter. However, Counsel may advise that the client's case is a strong one and would be likely to succeed. It may then be arranged that the Counsel concerned will, in fact, draft the pleadings, present the case and act as advocate in the arbitration proceedings. When a party is a firm or corporation it is even more likely that solicitors and Counsel will have been consulted at some stage before arbitration proceedings are initiated or defended.

It is worth repeating that neither party has to be represented in arbitration proceedings by a lawyer or any other advocate. It is entirely within the discretion of any party whether to appear in person or to be represented and, if so, by whom. It is within the discretion of the arbitrator whether to condone the involvement of Counsel by certifying: 'Fit for Counsel' in any order or in the award itself – or by declining to do so.

The arbitrator may himself decide (or be requested by the parties) to seek legal advice – either from Counsel or, in certain circumstances, by making a submission to the court on a question of law. For example, he can obtain advice from a solicitor (and, if necessary, Counsel) about the way to express his findings in an award. At the simplest level he may prepare a draft and ask his solicitor to look it over to ensure that he has not obscured his intentions or in any other way left the award open to challenge. The arbitrator will be also wise to obtain legal advice in drafting any submission to the court and, when the parties are represented by Counsel, they (Counsel) may be involved in the preparation of an agreed draft of any such submission. An arbitrator is entitled to that sort of assistance and will be wise to see that it is provided for in the arbitration agreement or, at least, in his acceptance of the appointment.

Another move in this field is when, at the request of the parties, the arbitrator obtains Counsel's opinion and then makes this available to the parties – as was done in *Gracomo Costa* v. *British Italian Trading* (1962). The arbitrator will normally pay for any legal services he has thus engaged and include the amount of such payment in the fees/expenses defined in his award.

It should not be overlooked that an arbitrator is himself empowered to consider written and/or oral submissions on questions of law – if necessary, at a special hearing for that purpose – and to publish his findings thereon in the award or, if appropriate, as an interim award.

Legal Aid

A party to arbitration proceedings cannot obtain financial assistance under the Legal Aid and Advice Act 1949 and other related provisions. It is not unknown, however, for the court to refuse an application under S.4 of the Arbitration Act 1950 when, for example, one of the parties would be prejudiced by his inability to obtain legal aid if such an application were granted – see *Fakes* v. *Taylor Woodrow* (1972).

Professional/Technical Advice/Assistance

Most professional/technical practitioners find that their first contact with formal arbitration or litigation proceedings or public enquiries is in the role of an 'expert' – initially advising behind the scenes and later, possibly, attending as an 'expert witness' at a hearing. Possible settings for such activities include proceedings in the High Court, County Court, the Land Tribunal, planning appeals and public enquiries. Needless to say, in these as well as in other circumstances, there are 'horses for courses'. The function of experts is to provide independent opinions based on the facts of the matter/s in dispute. Such opinions should be confined within the particular expert's qualifications and experience as applied to the features of a particular case – about which he will have to inform himself and/or be briefed by others. The role of an expert is exercisable in three stages: qualifying to give evidence in a particular case, preparing a 'Proof of Evidence' and, when necessary, giving evidence at a hearing.

Having made himself aware of the nature of the dispute and the particular question/s about which his opinion is required ('the material questions'), the expert should prepare a Proof of Evidence – a formal report which sets out

(a) his qualifications and relevant experience;
(b) the general background to the dispute in so far as this is necessary in relation to the material question/s;
(c) the material question/s;
(d) his opinion about the way in which the material question/s should be answered;
(e) the reason/s for such opinion.

There is no prescribed format for a Proof of Evidence and, provided he includes the main ingredients mentioned above, each expert can adopt his own style and ingenuity of presentation. The underlying implication of a Proof of Evidence is that the expert who produced it is prepared to testify accordingly at the hearing. A typical presentation is shown in (5), Part III.

An expert's fees/expenses are payable by the party who engages him and who, of course, hopes that he will be more expert and, therefore, more convincing in support of his case than any expert called by the other side. However, although an expert is engaged and paid by a particular party, he (the expert) must realise that at a hearing his role is to assist the arbitrator (or judge) in coming to a right view of the facts – whatever they are and however they may affect the interests of the party by whom he is engaged.

Other roles which professional/technical practitioners are sometimes required to fill are those of 'umpire' and 'assessor'. The role of umpire is defined in the 1950 Act and can be seen to be that of an arbitrator – albeit his appointment is by the arbitrators in a two-arbitrator-plus-umpire combination. It is not usual to find an assessor sitting with an arbitrator because the arbitrator himself is often chosen for his professional/technical knowledge of the sort of matters in dispute. Assessors are sometimes found on other tribunals, including courts of law, where a judge sits as the president with one or more professional persons to assist him with the assessment of technical matters. In the Admiralty Division of the High Court, for example, the presiding judge often has a marine expert sitting with him as an assessor – and there are many other similar situations. As such, assessors are engaged by the court (not by the parties) and their fees are paid by the court.

A further development in the role of the expert is by acting as 'lay-advocate' when, as a non-legal agent, he prepares and presents the case for one of the parties. When acting as such, the lay-advocate should ensure that he has his principal's agreement to the general strategy and presentation he proposes to adopt – bearing in mind the possibility of withdrawing at any stage rather than risking a charge of negligence. He should take courage, however, from the decisions of the courts already mentioned in *Rondel* v. *Worsley* and *Saif Ali* v. *Sydney Mitchell.*

There is no reason why the same person should not act as expert witness and lay-advocate in the same case but, in practice, this could be undesirable in other than the simplest sorts of disputes. In this context it is pertinent to note what has often been said – that a lawyer (or, for that matter, any other professional man) who advises himself may have a fool for a client.

Another role for the expert can arise when, if the parties so agree (in the arbitration agreement or otherwise), an arbitrator enlists the services/advice of an independent consultant. For example, if the matters in dispute include questions of measurement and valuation of building work and the arbitrator happens to be an architect, it is understandable that in certain circumstances he may need the opinion of an independent quantity surveyor to guide him on such matters. This would not be necessary when enough information comes out of the evidence presented by the parties to give him a good idea as to where the right answer lies but, in any such case, the final decision lies with the arbitrator. Incidentally, an expert witness can adduce details (e.g., measurements/calculations) compiled by others (e.g., his staff) for which he accepts responsibility.

The Preliminary Meeting

After confirming his acceptance of the nomination, and thereby completing the formalities related to his appointment, the arbitrator's usual first move is to convene a preliminary meeting at which he can clarify the issues, if necessary, and discuss with the parties how they wish to proceed. It is essential, at all stages, for the parties to follow a parallel procedure which they either agree between themselves or, in any event, accept as ordered by the arbitrator. At the preliminary meeting the parties should either attend in person or by any representative ('agent') whom they authorise to do so. In a building case, the client could be represented by his architect and the contractor by a member of his own staff or, on either side, by technical or legal advisors specially engaged to do so.

Prior to the preliminary meeting, the arbitrator knows very little about the matter apart from the names of the parties and the general idea of what the dispute is about. He will not know the details of the case or by whom the parties are or will be represented. All such matters have to be clarified including, perhaps, the question: what is the dispute about? As previously suggested, it is at this stage that it might be necessary for the arbitrator to help the parties to identify precisely the matter/s in dispute. Although he should not then attempt to force a 'hearing' of all the details he should find out, at least, whether they have agreed what it is they disagree about. And if, in the process, the arbitrator detects that the parties have been helped to narrow down or even to eliminate the differences between them he can and should encourage them to reach a settlement then and there, or as soon as possible thereafter, instead of taking it for granted that they intend to prolong the proceedings to the ultimate and, perhaps, bitter end.

In any case, it does no harm if the arbitrator expresses the hope that the parties will continue, without prejudice, their efforts to resolve their differences. And that, if they are able to do so, they should request him to issue an award 'by consent' accordingly.

Assuming that there is no possibility that the parties can settle the dispute at that stage, the arbitrator should ask about their intentions with regard to the pace (timing), preparation and presentation of their respective cases. Other details which the arbitrator should clarify at the preliminary meeting or, in any case, before the hearing include such questions as whether the parties are to be represented and, if so, by lay-advocate, solicitor or Counsel at the hearing. Also, how many 'experts' each party proposes to call and, if necessary, he should limit the number when, for example, an individual or a small firm is in dispute with a large and powerful organisation. In any case, by the time the arbitrator has heard one and possibly two experts on each side there is seldom any point in bringing others to cover the same ground.

At this stage, also, it may be prudent to enquire whether the parties, or either of them, require the arbitrator to support his findings by stating his reasons in the award. Then, if lawyers are present, he could ask whether it is evident that any question of law is likely to be a substantial element in the proceedings; also, whether and, if so, why it is proposed to submit any evidence by affidavit or on commission.

It may be also relevant to discuss whether a verbatim record of the proceedings should be taken by a shorthand writer or tape-recorder – and whether such records should be transcribed. The parties may compromise by agreeing that a record will be made but not transcribed unless a particular reason for doing so becomes clear at a later stage. This is sensible because the full operation can be very expensive. The question of a physical inspection by the arbitrator can also arise. If the dispute includes allegations of sub-specification goods/services/workmanship – or anything else that requires an inspection by the arbitrator – it would be useful to discuss and agree at what stage that inspection should be made. Generally, the right time for an inspection is said to be at the close of the hearing when the arbitrator has heard all the contentions by each side. Then, when he goes to see, he knows specifically what to look for. Even so, the timing of such inspection should be discussed and agreed at the preliminary meeting because, in particular cases, it might be appropriate for the inspection to be made at an earlier stage of the proceedings – even, perhaps, before the hearing takes place.

Another question which the arbitrator can helpfully raise since the 1979 Act came into force is whether the parties are aware of and/or have considered their options to enter into an exclusion agreement in respect of judicial review by the court on questions of law. This is the subject of S.3 of the 1979 Act – and reference is also made to it in Chapter 3. Then, if necessary, the arbitrator can assist the parties in entering into an agreement which embraces this provision as well as any others which may need to be tidied-up.

Subject to any agreement between the parties, the arbitrator has to decide at or soon after the preliminary meeting the periods he should allow for the interlocutory proceedings; in any case, he should always tend to be generous and can, in addition, give liberty to apply for an extension of time if that is found to be necessary by either party. By translating periods into dates, the arbitrator can set up a date-table and this is then made the subject of an order. In fact, the arbitrator will usually include in his first order his directions about these and other preliminary matters.

If, during the preliminary meeting (if not before) it becomes evident to the arbitrator that he has had some previous dealings with either party or others who are or will be involved in the proceedings he should declare this and give the parties the opportunity of confirming his appointment in the light of such disclosure. It is better to grasp that sort of nettle sooner rather than later when a question could be raised by one of the parties after the proceedings have reached an advanced stage. Even so, once his appointment is effected, the arbitrator cannot be removed except by mutual agreement or by order of the court.

Once the arbitrator is appointed, all communications and documents issued by him or either of the parties as part of the arbitration proceedings should be issued simultaneously to the others. Thus, orders by the arbitrator should be sent to each party and any letter or document issued by either party must be likewise sent to the other party and to the arbitrator. This is another matter to be mentioned at the preliminary meeting and confirmed in the arbitrator's first Order of Directions. At the same time, the parties may be involved in related 'without prejudice' discussions and/or communications without informing the arbitrator.

Arbitrator's Directions/Orders

Having ascertained the general position at the preliminary meeting, or otherwise, the arbitrator should issue his first Order of Directions – setting down the procedural framework within which the arbitration is to be conducted. All directions by the arbitrator should be issued either on the basis of consent by the parties or in accordance with his own decision after hearing the conflicting submissions (if any) of the parties. He will always attempt, as far as possible, to proceed on the basis of consent; his chief aim should be to assist the parties in the way and at the pace which they may have jointly agreed and, by so doing, help to narrow down the areas of disagreement as much as he possibly can. Hopefully, therefore, although the parties are in dispute they will at least be able to agree the way in which they are going to proceed to settle the matter. If such agreement is possible, well and good; but things do not always happen quite like that because, to some extent, one of the parties may refuse to co-operate and otherwise seek to obstruct the proceedings. In those circumstances the arbitrator must issue his directions with firmness while being fair to both parties.

The arbitrator's first Order of Directions should include his stipulations about general procedure and, if appropriate, a timetable (meaning 'date-table') related to the interlocutory proceedings – i.e., the exchange of Pleadings etc. Other events to be included in such date-table are the listing of relevant documents which are or have been in the custody, possession or power of the parties and the arrangements for discovery and inspection by each party of the documents in the possession of the other. It is not usual for the arbitrator to specify the date/time/place of the hearing in his first Order; he may do so, of course, but it is more realistic to defer that decision to a later stage. A typical example of a First Order of Directions is included as (4) in Part III.

Endorsements on Orders

Every Order of Directions (other than a Peremptory Order) should normally include the endorsement: 'Liberty to Apply'. This gives either party the right to apply for any term of that Order to be amended. For example, the stipulated date-table may be affected by the time taken to comply with a request for 'Further and Better Particulars'. Normally, the arbitrator should also add: 'Costs of this application to be costs in the reference'. This makes it clear that the costs incurred in applying, discussing with the arbitrator and complying with his directions shall be admitted as costs in the arbitration proceedings. The costs of the parties will be reflected in their respective bills of costs and the arbitrator's will be included in the charges stated in the award in respect of his fees and expenses. Then, in the light of what he learns at the preliminary meeting, the arbitrator should use his discretion about condoning the intention of either party to be represented by Counsel. He can express this by including (or omitting) the phrase: 'Fit for Counsel' when issuing his Orders. The practical effect of omitting so to certify is that the cost of engaging Counsel will not be admissible as part of the taxed costs payable by either party to the other.

Without claiming to be exhaustive, the foregoing comments will help to indicate the broad framework within which the arbitration proceedings get their shape, direction and timing. One result from the initiation of arbitration proceedings is that it may get the parties moving after having been deadlocked. The arbitrator should never attempt to stampede them, however; he can try to get them to agree the sort of date-table described but, unless the parties disagree between themselves and either of them applies to the arbitrator for a ruling, he should accommodate their wishes. Even after issuing an Order he must always be open to an application for a variation and to grant it if not opposed by the other party. On the other hand, the arbitrator should strictly enforce the date-table if one of the parties complains that the other is adopting what are known as 'delaying tactics'. This sometimes happens when a party is not sure of his position and would rather defer the final day of reckoning.

Pleadings

'Pleadings' is the generic term used for the documents prepared by and exchanged between the parties. They are not an essential feature of every arbitration but there should be a very good reason for dispensing with them. In some cases the arbitrator may ask to see copies of the pleadings as and when they are served so that he knows what is happening and may thus, if necessary, be the better able to deal with any submission by a party. In other cases, the arbitrator may not wish to see any documents until the exchange of pleadings has been completed. This is one of the procedural matters which should be clarified in his first Order. Irrespective of when he receives copies of the pleadings and other related documents, the arbitrator will merely note their general format and content without attempting to fully absorb all details at that stage. He can then listen with an open mind to what is said at the hearing.

Such documents should set out the facts (or alleged facts) upon which each party is relying to justify his position with regard to the matter/s in dispute together with the inferences based thereon; they should not attempt to give the supporting evidence or the arguments to be submitted at the hearing.

The main purpose of pleadings is to ensure that neither party is taken by surprise by anything of substance which is brought out at the hearing – thereby reducing the probability that delay and expense is incurred by a request from the 'surprised party' for an adjournment to consider any matter about which he has no previous notice. Accordingly, either party may request the other to supply 'Further and Better Particulars' in respect of any matter/s not fully explicit in any of the pleadings.

The documents normally exchanged as pleadings are

(a) *Points of claim*
A written statement by the claimant setting out the Points (Heads) of his claim, the amount of money claimed under each, the reasons for so claiming and a general indication of the evidence to be adduced at the hearing.

(b) *Points of defence*
A corresponding statement by the respondent purporting to show why the points of claim or any of them should not succeed.

(c) *Points of counter-claim* (if any)
The same as (a) above but served by the respondent.

(d) *Points of reply to defence to claim*
The final submission by the claimant in which he may comment on any matter/s raised in such defence and not adequately dealt with in the points of claim.

(e) *Points of defence to counter-claim* (if any)
The same as (b) above but served by the claimant.

(f) *Points of reply to defence to counter-claim* (if any)
The same as (d) above but served by the respondent.

By leave of the arbitrator (or of the court) the pleadings may be amended at any time before the hearing is closed. Typical presentations of pleadings are shown in Part III.

During the interlocutory exchanges, a request may be made by the recipient of an element of the pleadings for 'Further and Better Particulars' with regard to specific matters; for example, when points of claim or defence are thought to be not sufficiently explicit, or to be making allegations which do not logically follow from the facts to which reference is made. In such circumstances the usual action is to ask for the necessary further and better particulars to explain how a particular conclusion is reached. That might lead to the amendment of the pleadings first put in. For example, if the points of claim are thus challenged, the claimant may respond by re-phrasing part of the pleadings or by amending them in some other way. This is permissible in appropriate situations. Needless to say, such moves can be and, often are, used as delaying tactics which, unless they become manifestly unreasonable, may have to be consented to in order to eliminate any grounds for complaint about the time allowed for interlocutory matters. Other ways in which information can be elicited are by the use of 'interrogatories' – i.e. schedules with formal questions in one column and space for replies against them. Also, by 'discovery' and inspection of documents.

Discovery/Inspection of Documents

Further stages in the interlocutory proceedings may include

(g) *Discovery*
The disclosure, usually by exchanging lists, of the relevant documents which are or have been in the custody, possession or power of each party,

(h) *Inspection*
The exercise by either party of his rights to inspect any of the documents so listed by the other.

Subject to certain exceptions, all relevant documents which are or have been in the custody, possession or power of the parties must be declared by each party – whether or not he relies upon any of them in presenting his case. Exceptions are those which are held to be 'privileged' – e.g. correspondence passed between a party and his legal advisors in contemplation or pursuance of litigation or arbitration proceedings and other exchanges between the parties endorsed 'without prejudice'. Documents which are endorsed 'confidential' are not privileged as such; however, in certain circumstances, documents which contain details of a confidential nature – e.g. trade secrets – may be claimed to be privileged and, if necessary, the arbitrator may have to decide the status of one or more such documents. In those circumstances it may be easier to maintain confidentiality in arbitration proceedings than would be possible in open court.

An example of a list of documents for the purpose of 'discovery' is given in (11) Part III. When such lists have been exchanged, and subject to any time limits set by the arbitrator's date-table, each party may request to see any of the documents so listed by the other and, by mutual arrangement, obtain a copy of those he reasonably requires.

For convenience, all documents likely to be referred to in the proceedings should be grouped in appropriate 'bundles', each of which is labelled to indicate its contents (with an appropriate 'reference') and within which each item is numbered consecutively. Then, of course, each party should ensure that they and the arbitrator are supplied with identical documentation before the hearing.

The usefulness of what may be sometimes thought to be the pedantic numbering of paragraphs and sub-paragraphs in the documents which comprise the pleadings and the detailed numbered referencing of other documents in the 'bundles' cannot be over-estimated. The way in which the relevant documents are prepared and presented is highly important – particularly in the context of the actual hearing. If the arbitrator's task is made easier he is likely to be more relaxed and able to concentrate on the main issues instead of being fretted by the weakness of sloppy documentation and the absence of adequate means of cross-referencing.

The Reluctant Party

Reference has been made to the possibility that one of the parties may be reluctant to co-operate. For example, one party may be claiming payment and will be anxious to bring the matter to a conclusion as soon as possible while the other party, for reasons of his own, and being unwilling to pay, has no wish to expedite the time when he will be told he must pay. He may consider that money in hand is worth holding on to – especially in view of the high cost of finance. So, what happens? He may ignore the correspondence he receives from the other side; he may ignore the Orders and any other communications sent to him by the arbitrator; he may not turn up at the preliminary or any other meetings, in fact, he may look for and adopt all sorts of delaying tactics intended to obstruct the proceedings. Despite such non-co-operation, the arbitrator must maintain a 'reasonable' attitude and must give the reluctant party due opportunity for complying. For example, if on the appointed day for the preliminary meeting one of the parties (or his representative) turns up at the proper time and sits there, waiting, and there is no appearance by the other party or his representative, or any message to explain his non-arrival, it will become evident that he has ignored the notice to attend. The arbitrator, having given him enough time to arrive, should then abandon the meeting set for that day and, thereupon, issue a Peremptory Order by notice to both parties setting a resumed date – with the warning that if either party fails to attend or be represented on the adjourned date the proceedings will go on without him or, as it is formally described, on an *ex-parte* basis.

The arbitrator's common law power to act in such circumstances can now be reinforced by a warning that application may be made under S.5 of the 1979 Act for an Order of the High Court extending the powers of the arbitrator as may be necessary to enable him to proceed in the particular circumstances.

The same formalities can be applied in cases of non-compliance with other directions given by the arbitrator – always, however, on the basis of the arbitrator 'leaning-over-backwards' to be fair and reasonable to both parties.

Security for Respondent's Costs

Before discussing some general matters within the scope of this section, it should be mentioned that upon application by the other party, a company which is a plaintiff in a court action (or, if the court so orders, a claimant in arbitration proceedings) may be required in certain circumstances to deposit a sum as security for the costs of the defendant (or respondent) in accordance with the provisions of S.447 of the Companies Act 1948 and the relevant Rules of Court. This could prevent such plaintiff (or claimant) proceeding with his claim if his financial position is so precarious that he cannot comply with such an order – possibly, because of the very circumstances leading to the bringing of his action. For this and other reasons – e.g. that the claim appears to be genuine and is likely to succeed, and/or that the application for such security is made with the sole object of stopping the proceedings – the court may be reluctant to make such an order. This is illustrated by the case of *Sir Lindsay Parkinson* v. *Triplan* (1973) in which the CA upheld a decision of the HC which reversed the ruling by a Master who had ordered the stay of arbitration proceedings pending the depositing of such security by Triplan – the claimant. Thus, in arbitration proceedings, a similar application could be made to the court.

Summary Judgments

It has for some years been possible for plaintiffs in High Court proceedings to obtain summary judgment in respect of claims to which the defendant has no valid defence. This is by invoking what has become known as 'Order 14 Procedure' under RSC Order 14.

More recently, the court has acquired the power – under RSC Order 29 (Part II) – to order the defendant to make an interim payment of such amount it thinks fit pending the trial of the matter. By this means, the amount left owing to the plaintiff is reduced by such proportion as is evidently due and payable in any event.

No such powers are expressly conferred upon arbitrators and any moves towards such summary payments would be possible only by order of the court.

Interlocutory Settlement

The fact that parties have embarked upon an arbitration procedure, and may have even reached the preliminary meeting, does not compel them to go forward relentlessly to a formal hearing and its results. On the contrary, the parties should be encouraged to reach a settlement of their differences at any stage. It is not a rare occurrence for such settlement to be reached at or soon after the preliminary meeting – at which the arbitrator may have been able to assist the parties to concentrate their minds on a particular point. Other cases have been settled just before or during a hearing.

All sorts of variation of the standard theme are permissible by agreement. In other words, the parties and the arbitrator should have as their main concern the settlement of the matter so as not to prolong the proceedings unnecessarily. When the parties are laymen and appearing in person, the arbitrator's patience related to experience may enable him so to have his finger on their 'pulse' that he can sense when the right moment may have come for him to make an appropriate suggestion. However, as far as the arbitrator is concerned, the ways in which such interlocutory settlements are reached when the parties are legally represented are quite different. In those circumstances, any such initiative should be left to the legal advisor/s.

A corollary to any attempt to reach an interlocutory settlement can be the depositing of a 'sealed offer'. This is an option whereby a party, having had an offer of settlement refused by the other party at some stage of the proceedings, hands to the arbitrator (or, in certain circumstances, to the administering authority) a sealed envelope containing details of such offer. Any such envelope should be appropriately endorsed, of course, and a typical example of such endorsement is shown in (12), Part III.

Subsequently, when the award is decided in principle, and not yet published, the sealed envelope is opened. If the offer is then found to be more than the arbitrator has decided shall be paid by the offeror to the other party, the costs of the proceedings after the date of the refused offer are awarded against the party who refused it – irrespective of how they would otherwise have been awarded. In court proceedings the equivalent move involves the payment into court of the amount offered and neither the fact nor the amount of such payment is made known to the trial judge if it is made with denial of liability. In arbitration proceedings, the fact that a sealed offer exists is not always unknown to the arbitrator even though he may not know the details until the sealed envelope is opened.

One way of reducing the possibility that a respondent may feel he is prejudicing his case by the fact of putting in a 'sealed offer' was suggested by Mr (now Lord) Justice Donaldson who, as the judge in *Tramountana Armadora S.A.* v. *Atlantic Shipping Co. S.A.* (1978) had to deal with questions of liability for costs in consequence of such an offer having been deposited by the respondent in the related arbitration proceedings. That suggestion was that an arbitrator could invite (or order) the respondent to hand in a sealed envelope which contains *either* a copy of an offer-to-settle *or* a declaration that no such offer has been made. Thus, the handing-in of a sealed envelope would not be, *per se,* evidence that any admission of liability has been made by the respondent. His Lordship also pointed out that a second effect of a 'sealed offer' could be to limit the period in respect of which interest would be allowed on any amount subsequently awarded as damages.

6 The Hearing

Procedure

The procedure at a hearing is directed and controlled by the arbitrator with, preferably, the agreement of the parties. What follows, therefore, is broadly typical of what can happen but could be varied in particular cases.

The hearing is formally opened by the arbitrator. In doing so he makes some general comments with the object of clarifying the minds of all present and/or putting them at ease. For example, he may announce that, subject to circumstances, there will be a break for coffee at about 11.00 and that the lunch adjournment will be at about 1.00 with a resumption at, say, 2.30. In addition, the arbitrator should explain any other arrangements for the conduct of the case – including where he wishes the witnesses to sit when giving evidence and what is to be done about oath-taking.

The arbitrator could also give an indication of the time at which the hearing will be adjourned if not concluded on the same day. In deciding how long to sit on any one day, the arbitrator will be wise to bear in mind the judicial 5-hour day – particularly in extended hearings. There are limits – both physical and mental – in human ability to concentrate and to remain objective. However, it seems that maritime arbitrators can function under quite extraordinary conditions when necessary!

When, as will have been known from the interlocutory exchanges, only one of the parties is represented by a lawyer, the arbitrator may feel that it is also appropriate to indicate that he is mainly concerned with the establishment of the facts – adding, perhaps, that while he would be much obliged for any help which the lawyer representing the other side could offer in respect of legal points, he will otherwise conduct the proceedings without distinguishing between the advocates on either side.

It is sometimes asked whether all witnesses called by either side may be present in the arbitration room throughout the hearing. The typical answer is that, in general, all such witnesses may be present unless, for his own reasons, the arbitrator decides otherwise. In practice, it often happens that certain witnesses (especially experts) attend only in time to be called and, subject to the arbitrator's agreement, are released upon the conclusion of their evidence. Another important rule to remember is that a witness whose evidence has not been completed when at any time the hearing is adjourned is and should remain 'incommunicado' – even to his own side – until he has been 'stood down'. This rule is doubtless intended to protect a witness from being 'got at' during an adjournment and any serious breach of that rule could be regarded as 'contempt' and dealt with accordingly by the arbitrator – whose ultimate sanction is to have the matter reported to the court.

Are Arbitration Proceedings Privileged?

Another matter to which the arbitrator could usefully refer in his preliminary remarks is the question of 'privilege'. As most people know, whatever is said in Parliament, or in a Court of Law, is not actionable. However, Lord Denning has warned that arbitration proceedings may not be privileged in that sense. Therefore, if the arbitrator or any other participant in a hearing says anything slanderous it could be actionable. This is something for all concerned to bear in mind and, in any event, could help to avoid or reduce some of the 'heat' which might otherwise be generated.

Arbitrator's Note-Taking

The arbitrator will usually make notes throughout the hearing – whether or not an official record is being made and the pace of the proceedings will be governed to some extent by the nature and speed of such note-making. One very experienced maritime arbitrator has let it be known that he uses different colours of ink to distinguish between his notes of the respective submissions by the parties. Other helpful techniques include the use of marginal symbols to high-light particular features of the proceedings.

Claimant's Opening

After the arbitrator's preliminary comments the proceedings are begun by the presentation of his case by the claimant or his representative. Why, it may be asked, if the case has already been set out in the pleadings is it necessary to do this again at the hearing? In fact, the hearing is a rehearsal before the arbitrator of the *whole* story plus the submission of supporting evidence and argument – almost as though the pleadings did not exist. However, in presenting submissions to the arbitrator it is often convenient and quite in order to make reference to the pleadings. In addressing the arbitrator, for example, it could be stated: 'I will not quote all the figures to you, Sir, because they are set out in clause number (X) of the Points of Claim.' The arbitrator can then refer to that clause.

When his own case has been presented the claimant should deal with his defence to any counter-claim. The purpose of his opening address is, therefore, to inform the arbitrator

(a) why his claim should be met; and,
(b) why the counter-claim should be rejected.

Witnesses

Having concluded his opening address, the claimant (or his advocate) will support his contentions by calling witnesses and/or adducing documentary evidence. The general rules governing the presentation of evidence are mentioned later in this chapter. As he calls his witnesses, each of them is 'sworn', or makes an affirmation, if so required. When each witness has been examined (questioned) by his side – the 'examination-in-chief' – the other side has the opportunity of questioning him – the 'cross-examination'. This is the well-tried 'combat' method of arriving at the truth – whereby the witness's general competence, credibility and personality will register with the arbitrator. When, as often happens, the evidence of witnesses is in conflict, it is not correct to assume that either of them is telling deliberate lies. It is simply that one person's memory or opinion may be more reliable than another's. Everybody can be agreed, for example, that it was a blue car travelling North that collided with a red car travelling South; that is a matter of fact. But it is a matter of opinion when it is stated by a witness that the blue car was travelling at 60 miles per hour and that the red car was only going at half that speed. This illustrates the difference between facts and opinions and, when it comes to a question of conflicting evidence, it depends very much on the calibre of the witness as to whom an arbitrator, or a judge, will prefer to believe. This by-passes the question of what is and what is not admissible as evidence – to which, as stated, we will return.

When each witness has been cross-examined he can be re-examined by the party who called him – but only to clarify any point brought out by the cross-examination. The arbitrator may have to intervene if the other side objects that, in the re-examination, the party concerned (or his advocate) is taking advantage by re-presenting his evidence-in-chief.

Respondent's Reply

When the claimant's case has been presented the respondent addresses the arbitrator, and likewise calls and examines his witnesses who, in turn, will be subject to cross-examination – and re-examination if necessary.

Arbitrator's Intervention

Before any witness stands down the arbitrator may himself wish to question him about a point that has not come out clearly, or he may ask one of the parties to recall a witness in order to do so. The arbitrator is not allowed to call witnesses on his own account. He must proceed on the basis of the submissions by the parties and the evidence of the witnesses who testify before him.

It has been previously mentioned that the main purpose of the Pleadings is to avoid the risk that a party is taken by surprise by some material statement or evidence produced at the hearing by another party. Even so, it is not unknown for such surprise tactics to be adopted and, if so, the party who is thereby surprised may request the arbitrator to allow an adjournment so that he may examine such element of surprise and prepare his response to it. In such circumstances, to the extent that he considers it fair and reasonable to do so, the arbitrator should comply with such a request. At the same time, he should note and/or assess the extra cost incurred as a result of such an adjournment and take this into account when allocating the respective liabilities of the parties for the costs of the proceedings as a whole. Such extra costs can be said to have been 'thrown away'.

Closing Speeches

When the presentation of evidence has been concluded the respondent makes his closing address. In doing so he will try to persuade the arbitrator why the facts as he has presented them should be accepted and believed and why the case made by the claimant falls down for the reasons which he will there and then explain.

The claimant then makes his closing address and, in doing so, has the opportunity of arguing the merits of his own case and trying to dispose of the other side's contentions. It is a long-established rule that the person who originates the complaint, the claimant, has the last word.

At that stage the arbitrator could state that he is open to hear any further comment or information which either party may wish to place before him before the hearing is formally closed. This is not to encourage the repetition of anything said previously but to ensure that no-one is left with the feeling that he was not given an adequate opportunity of ventilating something relevant to the issue/s in dispute. He could then also invite the parties to submit to him their respective bills of costs so that, if so required, he may tax and include them as such in his award under the powers conferred upon him by the arbitration agreement and/or S.18(1) of the 1950 Act.

Close of Hearing

After that, the arbitrator will formally close the hearing – subject, it may be, to an adjournment for the purpose of an inspection. It is important that there should be the equivalent of an auctioneer's 'hammer-drop' so that the parties know that from that point no more can be said. Someone might suddenly remember, as he packs up his papers, that a particular point he intended to make had been forgotten. However, once the arbitrator has closed the hearing no more debate should be allowed. If an inspection is necessary the arbitrator will formally close the proceedings after that has been done – announcing, in any case, that his award will be published in due course. He may go so far as to indicate approximately how long he thinks it may take him to publish the award but he would be foolish to commit himself to a date for doing so and, officially, can take as long as he reasonably requires.

It is important to bear in mind that any necessary inspection of goods, commodities, workmanship or any other 'real evidence' should be made by the arbitrator only in the presence of all parties and/or their agents – having given them due notice of the day, time and place for so doing. If by the time appointed one of the parties fails to attend or be represented it would be prudent for the arbitrator to adjourn the inspection unless, in his discretion, he finds an overriding reason for not doing so. Another point to emphasise, is that the parties are present at such inspection for the sole purpose of answering such questions as the arbitrator may put to either of them in the presence of the other. The occasion must not be used in any way as a means of re-opening the hearing and, when he has satisfied himself and confirmed with the parties that he has seen all that is necessary, the arbitrator should formally close the inspection and withdraw from the scene.

It may be of interest to mention that the longest arbitration hearing on record lasted two hundred and thirty nine days – according to the *Guinness Book of Records* (1983). It was presided over by Mr Norman Royce and concerned a dispute arising in connection with the building of a new hospital at Peterborough.

Rules for Evidence

Evidence is information laid before a judge or arbitrator with the object of enabling him to identify and establish the facts of the matter/s in dispute. Such information may be 'oral' (given in person by a witness) or 'documentary' (by means of an original document) or 'real' (the thing itself). By leave, evidence may be also given by 'affidavit' or 'on commission'.

Evidence in arbitration proceedings is subject to the same rules as in the High Court. Oral evidence should be given on oath or affirmation unless there is general agreement to dispense with this formality. The standard procedure is for each witness to hold a Holy Book and, under the guidance of the arbitrator, to read aloud from a prepared card a statement such as: 'I swear by Almighty God that the evidence I shall now give will be the truth, the whole truth and nothing but the truth'. The 'holy book' may be the Bible – the whole or the Old or New Testament only – or any other book of fundamental significance to the religious beliefs of a particular witness. Alternatively, witnesses may 'affirm' by reading out another statement, similarly prepared and available, such as: 'I solemnly, sincerely and truly affirm and declare that the evidence I shall now give will be the truth, the whole truth and nothing but the truth'. In fact, some Christians prefer to affirm because our Lord forbade men to swear by heaven or by the earth or anything else because, as he put it: 'Let what you say be simply "yes" or "no"; anything more than this comes from evil'. (Matthew 5:37) Unfortunately, neither swearing nor affirming can be assumed to guarantee the veracity of any witness and the arbitrator has often to decide whether to believe a witness despite his/her oath or affirmation.

In giving their evidence, general witnesses can only deal with 'facts' while expert witnesses can, in addition to giving evidence about facts, offer their opinion about such facts. That is the main difference between the functions of a general witness and an expert at the hearing.

The first rule about evidence is that it must be relevant to the matter/s in dispute. Therefore, one of the most valuable qualifications for participating in arbitration proceedings, and any other related activity, is the ability to sort out the 'wheat' from the 'chaff'. One who can quickly appreciate the critical factor/s in a particular situation and is able to identify the relevant evidence will be able to ignore what is irrelevant and concentrate on what is vital – with, of course, a considerable saving of time. An arbitration hearing usually involves the attendance of several expensive people; time is of the essence and the arbitrator should not allow matters which are irrelevant to be pursued. On the other hand, he must be careful not to stifle what people want to say and it may be difficult, at times, for him to decide whether a line of questioning or a particular statement is relevant or not. The arbitrator must be prepared for that kind of dilemma and has to exercise his judgment to the best of his ability – erring, if at all, on the side of permissiveness.

Secondly, evidence of fact must be specifically what a general witness has himself seen or heard. Hearsay evidence – what he may have heard from someone else – is not generally admissible although, in certain circumstances, the Civil Evidence Acts allow such evidence to be given. The witness must be able to say, for example, 'I saw . . .' or 'I heard . . .' or 'I measured . . .' or 'I inspected . . .'. That is the general rule. It is permissible however, for a witness to say what he heard the opposing party or his agent say on a particular issue.

For example, if the dispute is about a claim for payment for extra building work, it would be relevant if a witness testified: 'We were standing at the North corner of the site; it was raining at the time and the architect instructed me to . . .'. That would be admissible because the architect is the agent of the employer.

It is a fact that many people find it very difficult to be completely objective about what they actually saw and heard. For example, somebody may arrive on the scene of a road accident a few minutes after the event. He sees the vehicles involved and a couple of injured persons nearby. His first question is likely to be: 'What happened?' A bystander tells him – and he can vividly imagine the impact. Later on, if that late-arrival offers or is asked to give oral evidence in court or elsewhere, it may be difficult for him to distinguish between what he actually saw and what he was told or imagined. Cross-examination often helps to clarify the mind of the judge or arbitrator in such situations even though the witness may be made to feel uncomfortable in the process.

Another important rule about evidence is that the party who makes an assertion has the burden of proving it. Sometimes somebody may make a statement and then say, in effect: 'Now, prove me wrong.' But there is no such legal obligation on the other party since no statement of material importance can be accepted by an arbitrator or judge unless it has been proved to be correct by the one who makes it. Whether or not the other side has been able to disprove it is beside the point.

There are also rules about the technique of questioning witnesses by the parties or their advocates although, in arbitration proceedings, those rules may not be applied quite as strictly as they would be in the courts. During the examination or re-examination of a witness, it is not permitted to ask what are called 'leading questions' – questions so phrased that the 'required' answer is thereby indicated.

However, leading questions are permitted in cross-examination and it does save time, for example, to put to a witness such a statement as: 'You told the learned arbitrator that it was a black and white collie that ran into the road and caused the accident'. 'Yes, I did.' This is merely a shortcut method of confirming certain facts as the spring-board for another question – which may either challenge what was previously said or take the questioning further.

A witness may be questioned not only about the facts of the case but also in such a way as to bring out whether he is truthful or whether he is professionally competent or whether he is a person of such character as to convince an arbitrator or judge that what he says is reliable. Sometimes, such questioning and, particularly cross-questioning, can be quite brutal and, since no one is without some cracks in his make-up, anyone can be embarrassed when exposed to the judicial spotlight. However, all such questions are permissible, within reason, if they are aimed at establishing whether a witness is to be believed or not, but the warning previously mentioned about 'privilege' should be always kept in mind.

General witnesses must normally give their evidence from memory but they may, by leave, 'refresh' their memory by reference to memoranda noted at the time of or soon after the event/s in question; experts can, in addition, refer to documents including any reports they have prepared. Memories may become a little dim about details, especially when figures are involved, but if a witness refers to any such memoranda or document it must be made available, upon request, to the other side unless it was previously 'discovered'. These points are mainly to do with oral evidence – that is, evidence given verbally by a witness before the arbitrator.

Another class of evidence comes under the general heading of 'documentary evidence'. One of the most important things to remember about documentary evidence is that the *original* document (i.e. best evidence) must be produced in each case. It is not enough to produce a copy and/or to bring before the arbitrator a witness who says, in effect, 'I saw a (nature of document) dated (date)'. In some circumstances, the parties may have to agree that a particular document shall be put in as a certified true copy of a missing original – without abandoning the principle that any documents relied on must be generally produced in their original form. And 'document' in this context includes any relevant agreement, contract, correspondence, drawing, specification, data and anything else of a written or printed nature to which reference is made in the proceedings. Some wag has gone so far as to point out that this could even include a tomb-stone! The Civil Evidence Act 1968 modified what had previously remained unaltered for a long time as the established rules of evidence. Among other provisions, this Act makes it permissible for films, tape-recordings, computer-processed material and other such features of modern life to be accepted as evidence – subject to the provisions of the Act. Such items come under the heading of 'documents' and are treated accordingly in the way referred to above.

Thirdly, 'real evidence' is 'the thing itself' which can be seen, examined and (if necessary) tested by or on behalf of the tribunal. Such evidence may be a personal injury, sub-standard goods or commodities, some unsatisfactory piece of work; it could be also said to include the performance of a witness under cross-examination – particularly when he/she is one of the parties to the proceedings.

As previously mentioned, evidence may be placed before a tribunal, by leave, by the submission of an 'affidavit'. This is a written statement made by a person who is competent to do so for the purpose of identifying a document or of setting down certain facts, figures and/or the opinion/s of that person about any relevant matter/s in the proceedings. The essential distinction between an affidavit and any other sort of written statement is that the former is 'sworn' by the deponent (the author) before a Public Notary (Commissioner for Oaths) who then signs the document to that effect. The submission of evidence by affidavit is sometimes adopted as a convenient method of receiving the evidence of a witness who cannot be reasonably expected to testify orally at the hearing and cannot, of course, be there and then cross-examined. A variation of this arrangement can be the granting of leave to admit such evidence subject to the right of the other side to require the deponent to attend for cross-examination at the hearing. In any case, the general question whether to allow affidavit evidence by particular witnesses and/or about any specific matter/s is entirely within the discretion of the arbitrator subject, of course, to any order of the court.

Evidence obtained 'on commission' is roughly equivalent to that supplied by means of an affidavit except that it is given orally to one or more 'commissioners' who then make and sign a statement to that effect. This is a convenient method of obtaining evidence when the witness concerned is overseas or otherwise unable to testify by other means. The procedure for this, subject to the approval of the judge or arbitrator, is laid down in RSC Order 39, Rules 1–2; it is also provided for in CCR Order 20 Rule 18.

It should be mentioned that the well-established facts and features of common life are deemed to be the subject of 'judicial notice' and, as such, do not require to be 'proved' every time they are referred to in litigation or arbitration proceedings. Otherwise, the time taken up by such proceedings would be enormously greater than it already is.

And finally, in this chapter, it is worth mentioning that the arbitrator has general powers to order the preservation of evidence – a matter which is often particularly relevant to what is referred to above as 'real evidence'.

7 The Award, Costs and Damages

Awards: Generally

Essential features of a valid award are that it is in writing and signed by the arbitrator in the presence of a witness who also signs to that effect. In addition, the award must be

1 relevant – by complying with the terms of the Reference and not exceeding them;
2 certain – by being consistent and unambiguous in its contents;
3 complete – by dealing with all questions referred and (subject only to over-ruling by the court) disposing of all matters in dispute.

Sometimes an award is deficient because, while dealing with the salient points, it fails specifically to deal with others mentioned in the reference. This could be because the arbitrator thought that certain matters had been dropped by the wayside but, if they are scheduled in the arbitration agreement, or otherwise included in the matters referred to him, he must deal with them in his award. After that they become *res judicata* and cannot be raised as issues in any other proceedings. Conversely, an award must not deal with any matters not referred to the arbitrator and, furthermore, it should not award any greater sum than is claimed – specifically or by inference. Guidance for the drafting of awards is given in Part III.

Interim Awards

Discretion is given to an arbitrator by S.14 of the 1950 Act to issue one or more interim awards before he issues his final award. An interim award may be a convenient means, for example, of settling one or more preliminary points (e.g. regarding respective liabilities) before proceeding to deal with other questions (e.g. with regard to quantum) – about which, at that stage, the parties could themselves reach an agreement to be incorporated in the final award 'by consent'. Another purpose in issuing an interim award could be to establish a basis on which to apply to the court for a ruling on a point of law in accordance with the provisions of the 1979 Act. In general, the content and format of interim awards follows, *mutatis mutandis,* that of final awards and the same principles apply.

Reasons

In making his award under the 1950 Act, an arbitrator in England and Wales was not obliged to state the reasons for his decision/s. There could be exceptions to that rule if the parties previously agreed and the arbitrator concurred in advance of accepting his appointment that reasons would be given. That was an exceptional arrangement and a common compromise, particularly in maritime arbitrations, was for the arbitrator to give his reasons as Notes in a separate but related document on the understanding that such notes would not be used in any subsequent proceedings related to the award. To make the position quite clear, such notes were often dated one day after (or before) the date of the award itself.

In his Alexander Lecture to the Institute of Arbitrators in 1974, Lord Denning (then Master of the Rolls and senior judge in the Court of Appeal) referred to the absence of reasons in arbitrator's awards. He pointed out that arbitrators, at that time, had one great advantage over judges in that, like juries, they did not have to supply the reasons for their decisions. An award that gives no reasons, he said, is virtually unchallengeable. He referred to a famous statement by Lord Mansfield: 'Consider what you think justice requires and decide accordingly, but never give your reasons, for your judgment will probably be right, but your reasons will certainly be wrong.' It is undoubtedly true that one very often develops a conviction about the right answer to a particular problem but, when asked to explain the reasons for feeling that way, it is not easy to do so – at least, not convincingly. Thus, as every parent knows, when reasons are given they may very well be proved to be illogical or, at least, challengeable even though the basic decision is itself correct. Subsequently, the 1979 Act introduced a reform whereby an arbitrator may be required by the arbitration agreement, or by order of the court, to supply the reasons for his award in such detail as may be necessary and adequate to enable the court to consider a question raised on appeal. Even so, it should be remembered that the giving of reasons does not require a full disclosure of the *reasoning* by which the arbitrator's decision has been reached.

Costs

An award must also allocate responsibility for paying the costs of the proceedings – that is to say, the costs incurred by the parties and the arbitrator's charges. If the arbitrator so feels, the award should also include the statement 'Fit for Counsel' – whereby he certifies that the parties were justified in briefing counsel (if, in fact, they did so), to prepare their respective cases and present them at the hearing.

The total cost of arbitration proceedings falls into two main categories, namely – the costs incurred by the parties in preparing and conducting their respective cases, and the arbitrator's charges. The costs so incurred by the parties are often referred to by such terms as: 'Costs in the Arbitration', 'Costs in the Reference', 'Costs in the Cause', 'Costs in the Action'. Before the recovery of any such costs can be enforced by one party against another, they must be agreed as between the parties or, in default of such agreement, they can be 'taxed'. Such taxation can be done by the court, upon application, or by the arbitrator under S.18 of the 1950 Act and prescribed in the award.

The arbitrator's charges are known as the 'Costs of the Award' and include his fees in accordance with the basis previously settled between him and the parties, plus the expenses he has properly and reasonably incurred in connection with the proceedings, plus VAT (if appropriate). The amount payable in respect of the Costs of the Award and by whom they are payable is determined by the arbitrator and stipulated in the award. When, as not infrequently happens, a dispute is settled by agreement and the arbitrator is not, for one reason or another, involved in such settlement or the issue of an award 'by consent', his account may be sent to the parties on a 'joint and several' basis.

In this context, the term 'costs' does not include the 'damages' payable by one party to the other in respect of the matter/s referred to in the claim or counter-claim in the arbitration proceedings. The general formula is that 'costs follow the event' – which is legal jargon meaning 'loser pays all'. There may be exceptions to that when, for example, the arbitrator feels that the party who has won, or has mainly won, has wantonly delayed the proceedings or has otherwise unnecessarily taken up time and, therefore, incurred additional costs in the proceedings. In such circumstances, the arbitrator has it within his power to award a proportion of the costs against each party, or he may state that the costs up to or from a certain date or point in the hearing are awarded against one party and the rest are awarded against the other. The need to make such an allocation of responsibility for meeting the costs can also arise from the 'sealed offer' procedure mentioned above. Alternatively, the arbitrator may state that he makes no order as to costs – meaning that each party bears and pays his own. The arbitrator is free to exercise any such option he thinks is just and equitable.

When an umpire has to act after two arbitrators have disagreed, his award should state specifically the fees due to himself and to the arbitrators, distinguishing between the fees payable to the latter as arbitrators up to the date of their disagreement and, subsequently, as advocates.

An arbitrator under S.92 of the County Courts Act 1959 is paid his fee and expenses out of the deposits which the Clerk of the Court will have required from both parties. The party who wins has his deposit returned and any balance due to the losing party is returned to him.

Publication of Award

The timing of the publication of his award is at the discretion of the arbitrator. Having 'published' it he notifies the parties that it is available to be taken up on payment of his charges – which are also then stated. Either party can pay such charges – by post or by going personally to the appointed place – and take up the award. If it is then discovered that the arbitrator's charges are in fact payable by the other party the matter has to be sorted out in the general squaring-up which ensues.

The foregoing references to the arbitrator's award are particularly applicable to circumstances in which the arbitrator has come to a decision and, in effect, imposes it upon the parties – one of whom is likely to be disappointed while the other, to an equal and opposite extent, is elated.

The same principles are also applicable in other cases when, at some stage of the proceedings, the parties decide between themselves the terms upon which they agree to settle the matter/s in dispute which were referred to the arbitrator. In these circumstances, the proper course is for the parties to inform the arbitrator of the terms of their agreement so that he may issue an award 'by consent of the parties' instead of on the basis of his own adjudication. Otherwise, the features of a 'by consent' award and its related procedures are parallel to those of any other award.

Occasionally, for one reason or another, parties fail to inform the arbitrator that they have agreed to settle and this, to say the least, is grossly discourteous on their part. When he discovers the position, the arbitrator could inform the parties

1 that the position has come to his notice and he is prepared to issue a 'By Consent' award upon request; and/or
2 that in default of such request within (say) twenty eight days an account for his fees/expenses will be sent to the parties on a 'joint and several' basis.

Upon publishing his award, the arbitrator automatically becomes *functus officio* and, subject to certain matters arising, has no longer any status in the case. The time-limit for challenging awards under the 1950 Act was six weeks from the date on which the parties were notified of its publication. Now, under the 1979 Act, this period is reduced to 21-days. In the absence of any such challenge, it then becomes fully binding and enforceable – as confirmed in *Middlemiss and Gould* v. *Hartlepool Corporation* (1973).

An arbitrator has a lien on the arbitration agreement and the award – but not on any related document – pending payment of his charges. If such lien is exercised the court may, on application, order that the award is delivered to the applicant upon paying the amount of such charges into court. This would be for the purpose of having them taxed, subject to what may have been previously agreed in writing between the arbitrator and the parties. But, what happens if the 'losing' party fails to comply with the terms of an award? Upon application to and by leave of the court an award can be enforced in the same way as a judgment of the court and at that stage, if not before, the aggrieved party should seek legal advice.

Taxation of Costs

Upon application, the costs of the parties can be 'taxed' by the court in accordance with a comprehensive set of rules and schedules of charges issued under RSC Order 62 – in which Rule 2(1) makes the order applicable, *inter alia,* to arbitration proceedings. This being so, it is important that an award makes clear the basis on which the costs of one party are to be met by the other/s – e.g. 'party-and–party' or 'solicitor-and-client' – so that the appropriate scale can be applied. Thus, the costs incurred are subject to scrutiny by the court tax-master if one or both of the parties so wish and it should be noted that the scales are such that even the 'winner' might not recover all that he has expended. This, however, should not deter the arbitrator from refusing to condone the cost of any expenditure which, in his opinion, was unreasonable.

Even in the simplest sort of proceedings, lay-advocates should not attempt to grapple with post-award questions which may arise between the parties with reference to the taxation of costs. At that stage the best advice they can give their client is to consult a solicitor.

The arbitrator's fees and expenses are subject to such taxation only to the extent that they have not been agreed by the parties in advance and/or that they are not 'taxed and settled' in the award. If an arbitrator or umpire has to add an element for VAT to his service charges this must be clearly indicated in his award. Then, if so required, he should issue a 'tax invoice' for the total amount so payable by either (or both) of the parties as may be appropriate.

Damages

'Damages' is the amount held to be payable by or on behalf of a person who causes 'damage' (injury, loss or expense) as restitution to the person who has suffered it or to his dependents.

As a legal doctrine, at least, there is no 'damage' which cannot be compensated by financial restitution despite the fact that such damage may itself be irreversible. Therefore, the fundamental principle governing the assessment of damages is that the sufferer be restored to the position in which he would have been but for the damage suffered or, alternatively, provided with the means of compensating such damage.

Damages which can be calculated (e.g. commercial losses, loss of earnings, medical fees) are 'special damages'; those in respect of loss or damage which cannot be quantified (e.g. for personal suffering or inconvenience) are 'general damages' and have to be assessed. The 'measure of damages' is the amount so payable by agreement of the parties or, failing such agreement, by order of a judge or an arbitrator.

Derisory and Exemplary Damage

In certain circumstances, a party may win his claim on a technicality while, at the same time, demonstrating to the court or arbitrator that in all the circumstances he has not acted fairly and reasonably or that his action was brought vexatiously or maliciously. This could be reflected by his being awarded such a nominal sum as to be 'derisory damages' and, furthermore, he could be required to pay a proportion of the costs of the action. In other circumstances, a court (but not an arbitrator) may award 'exemplary damages' – which includes an (extra) amount to be paid by a wrong-doer as a punitive measure and a discouragement to others.

Interest

Assuming that the arbitrator decides that a party is entited to succeed in his claim for interest on any amount due to him, the question arises about the rate/s which should be applied in calculating the amount of such interest. Acting on the principle that the award of damages should restore the injured party to his 'pre-damaged' position, the arbitrator can take note of the actual interest paid by the claimant on any overdraft during the material period or, if no such over-draft was incurred, the average commercial rate/s of interest over that period could be applied. The arbitrator's power to award interest, previously implied, is specifically defined in a new section (19A) inserted in the 1950 Act by S.15(6) of the Administration of Justice Act 1982. This power is limited to the granting of simple interest – but is without prejudice to any other power to allow interest. Such interest, it must be emphasised, is applicable only up to the date of the award for, in default of the award being honoured within a reasonable time, any further claim for interest has to be related to that which the court will allow in respect of a judgment debt – which may be considerably less than the actual cost of an on-going overdraft at the bank and thus, *per se,* is no real incentive towards settlement.

Misdirection by Arbitrator

Specific examples of misdirection/misconduct by an arbitrator include – attempting to deal with matters not referred, awarding more than is claimed, issuing an award which is uncertain or ambiguous, refusing to state a case under the (now superseded) provisions of the 1950 Act, attempting to delegate any part of his authority, appearing to have a personal interest or involvement in the matters in dispute, accepting hospitality or any other form of gift or bribe from either of the parties to the dispute.

Conclusiveness of Final Awards

As confirmed by Mr (now Lord) Justice Donaldson in *Tradex Export SA* v. *Andre and Cie SA* (1978), arbitrators are in the same position as the Employment Appeals Tribunal and the Restrictive Practices Court in that while their decisions on questions of fact are final, their decisions on questions of law may be reviewed by the court.

Impeachment of Award

Under RSC Order 73 Rule 5(1), as amended by RSC (Amendment No. 3) Order (SI 1979 No. 522) any application to impeach (challenge) a published award must be made to the court within 21 days. Compared to the previously stipulated period of 6 weeks this could be a difficulty for an aggrieved party in certain circumstances but prior to the expiry of such stipulated period the following moves are possible

(a) the arbitrator may, in accordance with S.17 of the 1950 Act, correct any 'slips' in his award – such as typographical errors and any non-critical mistakes in the final engrossment;
(b) an application may be made by the parties, or either of them (subject to the limitations of the 1979 Act) and, consequently, the court may remit an award to the arbitrator with a direction that it be amended in certain respects – with or without indicating the form of or content of any such amendment/s. In such circumstances the arbitrator is required to re-open the proceedings (but only in respect of the matter/s so remitted to him) and to publish an amended award which, under S.22(2) of the 1950 Act, must be done within three months unless the court orders otherwise;
(c) upon application by the parties, or either of them, the court may set aside an award in certain circumstances – such as finding that it has been improperly procured, the arbitrator or umpire has misconducted

himself or the proceedings or (subject to the parties not having entered into an 'exclusion agreement' under S.3 of the 1979 Act) if the award contains some obvious error of law on the face of it. If an award is set aside the arbitrator has no further part in any subsequent proceedings; furthermore, in cases of flagrant misconduct, the arbitrator (or umpire) concerned may be laible to return any fees paid to him in accordance with such award;

(d) the parties, or either of them may apply to the court for leave to apply for a ruling on a point of law arising on an award – again, subject to the limitations of the 1979 Act. Any application under S.92 of the County Courts Act 1959 to have an award set aside must, in accordance with CCR Order 37 Rule 7 be made within six days of the receipt of a copy of the judgment by the party concerned. There is no appeal against the arbitrator's findings, as such, since the only grounds on which the judge or registrar can consider setting aside such award are that the arbitrator had no jurisdiction or that he was evidently biased or that the award has an error on the face of it. Should such an application be refused an appeal can be made to the Court of Appeal subject to the provisions of S.108 of the said 1959 Act.

Although the remission and setting aside of awards by the court is not unheard of, it should be emphasised that such moves affect only an insignificant proportion of the total number of commercial arbitrations which are conducted over a given period.

8 Arbitration in Construction Contracts

Standard Forms of Contract

Examples of how arbitration agreements are incorporated in 'domestic' commercial contracts can be seen in the arbitration provisions of the standard forms of contract used in connection with the execution of construction works. These include: the JCT Standard Form of Building Contract and related Sub-Contract Documents, the ICE Conditions and the General Conditions of Government Contract Building and Civil Engineering Works (GC/Works/1) and, a more recent arrival, the ACA Form of Building Agreement. This is by no means a comprehensive list of all such standard forms in which arbitration provisions are incorporated. Similar provisions are also included in the standard terms of engagement under which professional consultants undertake commissions for their clients.

Other standard forms are available for use in connection with 'foreign' construction contracts. They are not dealt with here because their provisions, in some cases, extend into the sphere of international arbitrations and foreign law – which, as previously indicated, are too complicated for most non-lawyers to comprehend and implement without expert legal guidance. In any case, readers who may be particularly interested in the comments which follow are advised to consult the text of the respective documents.

The JCT Contract and Related Sub-Contract Forms

The concept of a standard form of building contract was first adopted by the publication, in 1903, of the document which resulted from a tri-partite agreement between the Royal Institute of British Architects, the Institute of Builders and the National Federation of Building Trades Employers of Great Britain and Ireland. Subsequently, the number and make-up of the sponsoring bodies was increased at various times until, by 1980, they comprised 3 professional bodies, 3 contractor and sub-contractor associations, 4 local government bodies plus the Scottish Building Contract Committee – and the CBI holding observer status.

The 1903 edition was followed by revised versions in 1909, 1931 and 1939 – all of which were generally referred to as 'the RIBA contract'. A further and major revision was published as 'The JCT Standard Form of Building Contract' in 1963 – thereby acknowledging that the generic term for the sponsoring bodies had become 'the Joint Contracts Tribunal'. The latest and quite radical revision was published by the JCT in 1980 as a 'package' comprising

(a) standard form of building contract available in various versions to suit the nature of the 'Employer' and to establish the role of the Bills of Quantities, if any – generally referred to as 'JCT '80';
(b) Standard Form of Tender for Nominated Sub-Contract Works (NSC/1);
(c) Standard Form of Employer/Sub-Contractor Agreement (NSC/2) for use when NSC/1 has been used;
(d) Ditto (NSC/2a) for use when NSC/1 has not been used;
(e) Standard Form of Nomination (NSC/3) for use only when NSC/1 and NSC/2 have been used;
(f) Standard Form of Sub-Contract (NSC/4) for use when NSC/1, NSC/2 and NSC/3 have been used;
(g) Ditto (NSC/4a) for use when NSC/1 and NSC/3 have not been used and NSC/2a has been used;
(h) Form of Tender for Nominated Suppliers (optional).

The main features of the arbitration provisions of (a) above remain substantially as they were in the latest revision of the 1963 editions. Those provisions have been extended, however, and are now incorporated, for the most part, in Article 5 of the 1980 form. Since an arbitration clause in conditions of contract is, in effect, an agreement within an agreement, this seems to be a logical tidying-up in the drafting process. Other relevant provisions, as in previous editions, are embodied in other clauses of the related Articles and Conditions. Parallel arbitration provisions are also incorporated in the documents mentioned above under (c), (d), (f), (g) and (h).

The arbitration provisions of the JCT '80 (main) contract form are related by Article 5.5 thereof to English law and, in particular, to the Arbitration Acts 1950 to 1979. This applies despite the fact that any party or the arbitrator may be a national of or a resident in a foreign state and wherever the Works are located. To make this clear, the exlusion of Scotland and Northern Ireland by S.34 of the 1950 Act is specifically overridden.

An interesting new feature of the current arbitration provisions is the authority given to arbitrators by Articles 5.1.4 and 5.1.5 of the main form and the parallel provisions in other related documents, subject to agreement by the parties, to hear and determine all related matters in dispute – whomsoever between – in combined proceedings which would otherwise have to be dealt with separately under the arbitration provisions of the main contract and one or more particular sub-contracts respectively.

Disputes in respect of the following matters can be referred to arbitration as/when they arise

1 the appointment of a new architect/S.O. (Article 3A/3B);
2 the appointment of a new quantity surveyor (Article 4);
3 the issue (or non-issue) of a particular architect's instruction (Article 5.2.2);
4 the issue or non-issue of a particular architect's certificate (Article 5.2.2);
5 the contractor's objection to a particular instruction (Clause 4.1);
6 the extension of time (Clause 25);
7 the effect of 'hostilities' (Clause 32);
8 the effect of 'war damage' (Clause 33).

Disputes in respect of the following matters are also referrable but not until after Practical Completion has been (or is alleged to have been) achieved, or the contractor's employment has been (or is alleged to have been) determined:

1 the adjustment of the contract sum (Clause 30.6.2);
2 the determination of Contractor's employment by the Employer (Clause 27);
3 the determination of Contractor's employment by the Contractor (Clause 28);
4 the determination of Contractor's employment (by either party) upon the outbreak of Hostilities (Clause 32);
5 the consequences of war damage (Clause 33);
6 the exclusion of any dispute about the Fair Wages provisions (Clause 19A) in relation to the statutory resolution of disputes arising on the Tax Deduction Scheme (Clause 31.9) and with regard to appeals to the VAT Commissioners (Clause VAT/3).

The arbitrator is authorised to exercise the same powers as the architect under the contract in respect of valuation and payment for the Works and the issue of any certificate, opinion, decision or notice and any other matter in dispute – irrespective of what may or may not have been previously issued. (Article 5.3).

Once it is established that a dispute or difference exists and, presumably, that it seems unlikely that an agreed settlement can be reached within a reasonable time, either party can give notice to the other requesting him to concur in the appointment of an arbitrator to hear and determine the matter/s in dispute. Then, if within fourteen days of such notice the parties have not been able to so concur, either of them can apply to the RIBA for an appointment to be made by the President or a Vice-President of that body. The same procedure is prescribed in the documents NSC/2 and /2a and, also, as an alternative, in NSC/4 and /4a although the first alternative under the latter is to apply to the RICS.

A further provision of the arbitration agreement expressed as Article 5, is that the parties will accept an award by the arbitrator as final and binding upon them (see 5.4). This may appear to be unnecessary in the light of S.16 of the 1950 Act, but, as previously mentioned, this is one of the matters about which the parties can, if they wish, express an alternative provision in their arbitration agreement.

The arbitration provisions of the Employer/Sub-Contractor Agreement (NSC/2 and /2a) are in Clause 8 of that document. Those of the Standard Form of Sub-Contract (NSC/4 and /4a) are in Article 3 of that document. In addition to providing for arbitration in parallel with the provisions of the (main) contract, Article 3 of NSC/4 and /4a provides for arbitration in respect of disputes about claims and counter-claims between the parties with regard, in effect, to 'set-off'.

Before leaving the disputes procedures specified in the JCT document, it should be noted that the Sub-contract Agreement (NSC/4 and /4a) maintains the provisions of the previous NFBTE/FASS/CASEC 'Green' and 'Blue' standard forms of sub-contract with regard to the procedure to be followed, if necessary, when a contractor proposes to set-off against any sum he should pay to a sub-contractor the amount of (in effect) a counter-claim against that sub-contractor. As previously, this provides for the matter to be referred to an Adjudicator who is required to investigate and adjudicate the matter on a *prima facie* basis without in any way prejudicing the freedom of an arbitrator with regard to the same matter. Also retained is the related provision for depositing the disputed amount with a Trustee/Stake-holder.

The ICE Conditions and Related Sub-Contract Forms

The ICE Conditions in current use are those of the Fifth Edition – first issued in June 1973 and amended in January 1975 – in which the provisions for the settlement of disputes appear as Clause 66(1). This provides, in effect, for disputes arising between the parties to be referred, in the first instance, to the Engineer under the contract. In so acting, however, the Engineer is not an arbitrator. Then, and only if the dispute has not been thus resolved, the aggrieved party can have a second bite at the proverbial cherry, so to speak, by requesting the other party to concur in the appointment of an arbitrator or, failing such concurrence, by applying for the appointment of such arbitrator by the President for the time being of the Institution of Civil Engineers (ICE). As to the related FCEC Standard Form of Sub-Contract, the arbitration procedure is in Clause 18 – which is parallel to that of the ICE Conditions without the requirement that any dispute is referred in the first instance to the engineer. It is further provided that, when a dispute arises between the contractor and the employer, the contractor may, in certain circumstances, join the sub-contractor in arbitration proceedings under the (main) contract – whereupon the arbitrator in those proceedings becomes 'the joint arbitrator'. The same provisions are made in respect of court proceedings.

Even so, there is a sense in which the respective arbitration proceedings (employer v. contractor and contractor v. sub-contractor) remain independent although interrelated. This is important with regard to any exclusion agreement/s which the respective parties may contemplate or execute and raises the question whether the publication of separate awards is required to deal with the respective references.

GC/Works/1 Conditions

Edition 1 of the *General Conditions of Government Contract for Building and Civil Engineering Works (Form GC/Works/1)* was published in November 1973 and thus became the successor to the similar document known as *CCC/Wks/1.* Edition 2 of the new document was issued in September 1977.

The arbitration provisions are contained in Clause 66 and express some interesting differences compared with those in other standard forms. For example, failing agreement by the parties about whom shall be the arbitrator, any matter/s in dispute are referrable to a person to be appointed by the President for the time being of one of the following: Law Society (or Law Society of Scotland), the RIBA, the RICS, the RIAS, the ICE, the IMechE, the IHVE, the IEE, the IStructE. The discretion about which of these bodies should be approached is vested in 'the Authority' (i.e. the statutory body in the role of employer) under the contract. All or any matters in dispute arising out of the contract may be referred to arbitration except those in respect of the Fair Wages provisions (Clause 51) and others in respect of which a decision by the Authority or by any other person is final and conclusive in accordance with other specific provisions of the contract. Matters specifically excluded from the scope of such arbitration provisions include

(a) the removal of anything brought to the site by the contractor or others acting for him (Clause 3(1));
(b) the evaluation of works covered up without due notice being given by the contractor (Clause 9(5): edition 1; Clause 9(3): edition 2);
(c) the adjustment of the contract sum under the variation-of-price clause (Clause 11G(4)(c));
(d) the compliance of materials etc. with specification requirements (Clause 13(3));
(e) the formalities related to partial possession before final completion of the Works (Clause 28A(6));

(f) the replacement of persons employed by the contractor in connection with the contract (Clause 36(3));
(g) fortnightly interim payments in certain circumstances (Clause 40(3));
(h) direct payment to sub-contractors and suppliers (Clause 40(5): edition 1; Clause 40(6): edition 2);
(i) the issue of certificates for interim payments and/or to register the date of practical completion (Clause 42(3));
(j) supplementary directions by the Authority in consequence of its determination of the contractor's employment for any reason other than default by contractor (Clause 44(2)(a)(vi));
(k) payment to contractor in respect of hardship related to such determination (Clause 44(5));
(l) the consequences of default by the contractor in controlling admission to the Works in accordance with the provisions of Clause 56 (Clause 45(c));
(m) the computation of the anticipated cost of superintendance and establishment charges necessary to complete the Works upon determination of contractor's employment under Clauses 45 or 55 (Clause 46(1)(e));
(n) disputes arising from allegations that the contractor is responsible for an offence under the Prevention of Corruption Acts 1889 to 1916 (Clause 55(3));
(o) the admission of persons to the site of the Works (Clause 56(4)).

Subject as provided, any other dispute/s may be referred to arbitration but, unless otherwise agreed by the parties, such matter/s cannot be referred until after the Works have been completed (or allegedly completed) or abandoned – or *the contract* has been determined. This last circumstance differs from the parallel provisions of other standard forms of contract in which reference is made to the determination of *the employment of the contractor.*

The clause is concluded by the insertion of alternative provisions with regard to the proper law of the contract – including the respective effects of the application of English or Scottish Law.

The ACA Form of Building Agreement 1982

The Association of Consultant Architects (ACA) published in October '82

(a) ACA Form of Building Agreement 1982;
(b) ACA Form of Sub-Contract 1982;
(c) Guide to the ACA Form of Building Agreement 1982;
(d) Relative Forms – i.e. Architect's Instruction, Interim Certificate (Payment), Taking-Over Certificate, Final Certificate.

Alternative procedures for the settlement of disputes are prescribed in Clause 25, from which the parties can select the one they wish to adopt at the time when the contract is executed. The first is a series of developments, as follows:

Stage I. Matters in dispute which arise at any time before the 'taking-over' of the Works with regard to

(a) the adjustment or alteration of the contract sum;
(b) the contractor's entitlement to an extension of time;
(c) whether the works comply with the contract documents;
(d) the employer's entitlement to terminate the contractor's employment,

can be referred to an adjudicator who is appointed *ab initio* and is thus available at short notice to step in as soon as the need arises. He is then required to

1 take note of and record the facts as they then exist, and,
2 give his decision within seven days.

In doing so, the adjudicator acts as an expert (not an arbitrator) and his ruling is pre-agreed by the contract conditions to be binding unless either party gives notice within twenty eight days that he requires the matter to be referred to arbitration. Any such arbitration cannot proceed until after the Works are taken over or the termination of the contractor's employment.

Stage II. Matters with regard to which the adjudicator's ruling is not given within the said time-limit or, if so given, is not accepted by either or both parties can (subject as provided) be referred to the arbitration of the same person who is named in the contract as the adjudicator or, if the parties so agree, to another person. The role and function of the erstwhile adjudicator or other person thus becomes that of an arbitrator under the Arbitration Acts 1950–79 and, as such, he can investigate and rule upon any matter in dispute and referred to him – not only those referrable to the adjudicator as such.

The second alternative provides for a similar procedure to the first, except that no adjudicator is named in the contract and his role/functions as defined in the first alternative are expanded in certain respects and allocated to the architect. Then, if necessary, the matter/s in dispute can be referred to an arbitrator – being a person (not the architect) who may be agreed by the parties or, in default of such agreement, 'appointed' by the chairman of the ACA upon application by one of the parties. Again, no such arbitration can take place before the Works have been taken-over.

The third alternative for which provision is made is for any dispute/s to be taken direct to court and settled there under English or Scottish Law as may be appropriate.

Clause 15 of the ACA Form of Sub-Contract provides two alternative means for the settlement of disputes – namely, arbitration and litigation – corresponding to the second and third of those available under the provisions of the ACA (main contract) Agreement.

With regard to the arbitration option under the said clause 15, the contractor or the arbitrator can require that any dispute between the contractor and the sub-contractor which may be related to a dispute between the contractor and the employer be heard by the same arbitrator as the one appointed to act under the (main) contract.

No specific provision is made in the sub-contract conditions for the appointment of an adjudicator but, by clause 15.4, any decision of the adjudicator under the (main) contract which is final and binding upon the contractor is also final and binding upon a sub-contractor – at least until after the Works are taken-over or the sub-contractor's employment has been determined.

9 Arbitration in Maritime Disputes

Scope for Disputes

Disputes in maritime operations can arise in connection with

(a) ship-building
(b) ship-operating
(c) salvage

As defined in S.742 of the Merchant Shipping Act 1894, a 'ship' is a water-borne vessel propelled by any means other than manually-operated oars or, it may be presumed, other such means of propulsion e.g. single-bladed or rotary paddles motivated by animal-generated energy. In 1894, however, the statutory definition would apply to vessels driven by wind and/or steam. Incidentally, and totally irrelevantly, another sort of 'ship' is the caviar-producing hybrid of the sturgeon family – mentioned in a gastronomic comment in *Arbitration* (October 1978).

Ship-Building Disputes

The circumstances in which the building of a ship is conceived and initiated are, *mutatis mutandis,* similar to those of construction projects in the fields of building and civil engineering. And, similarly, problems can develop into disputes with regard to the quality of materials/components, equipment, services and/or workmanship; also, with regard to non-completion or failure to deliver particular elements at particular stages or, in particular, by the prescribed completion date for the whole.

Ship-building contracts usually prescribe that disputes which arise and which cannot be otherwise resolved be referred to a technically qualified and otherwise acceptable marine engineer or other independent consultant who is thus empowered to investigate and adjudicate upon technical issues as/when they arise. The speedy resolution of such matters during the construction stage can be a critical factor and, even after delivery, it is to the ultimate advantage of the parties and others concerned to do so with the least possible delay. Exceptions to that can be seen in the reluctance of, say, the potential owner to take delivery of and pay the final instalment due on a new ship which, by that time, is surplus to his requirements; in such circumstances he may seek to delay settlement by allegations of default, in one respect or another, by the other party.

Certain issues which seem to hang upon a relatively simple question of fact, e.g. whether a particular break-down was due to sub-standard materials or workmanship – or, on the other hand, to improper operation or use of the vessel or any part of it, can become the subject of complicated legal arguments when liability for the consequences of such break-down is a secondary but, perhaps, the major issue. If so, it might be better for the parties to refer their dispute to an arbitrator who is a lawyer and before whom the technical evidence can be presented by technical experts.

Ship-Operating Risks/Disputes

Two or more of the following parties may be involved in a particular voyage: (a) ship-owner, (b) charterer, (c) cargo-owner/consignor, (d) cargo consignee – each of whom has different but related interests, rights and obligations. Relationships between (a) and (b) are usually defined in a type of contract called a 'Charter Party' – in which one of the governing clauses is, in effect, an arbitration agreement. A typical example of such a clause is –

> All disputes arising in the execution of this Charter Party to be referred to Arbitration in London. If the parties cannot agree on the appointment of a Sole Arbitrator, each party to appoint an Arbitrator and, in case they cannot agree, they shall appoint a third Arbitrator. The award of the majority to be final.

Such a clause, coupled with the fact that London has remained a popular 'locale' for the determination of maritime disputes, including those with a 'foreign element', has helped to establish the London Maritime Arbitrators' Association (LMAA) and the international reputation earned and enjoyed by its members for impartiality, speed and efficiency. Even when shipowners and others engaged in maritime operations are nationals of and/or based in foreign countries, their choice of 'Arbitration in London' implies that any dispute between them will be heard in London under English Law.

Because ships are mobile and, unlike land-based vehicles, not confined to physically-restricted 'traffic-lanes', they inevitably operate under a variety of risks – such as:

(a) collision with another ship or some natural or man-made obstruction;

(b) loss/damage/delay due to
  (i) fire, inclement weather and other perils,
  (ii) deterioration of cargo – particularly commodities,
  (iii) the action or inaction of others over whom the parties have no control,
  (iv) mechanical break-down,
  (v) negligence of the ship's master and/or his crew,
  (vi) other causes;
(c) war risks.

Subject to the provision of their trading agreements and the relevant legislation, the respective rights and obligations of the parties in any of the circumstances mentioned above are referrable, when necessary, to arbitration under English law within the scope of what is written above about commercial arbitration in general.

Salvage

Salvage, in the maritime context, means the rescue or retrieval of a ship and/or its cargo which, but for the intervention of the 'salvor' would have been a total loss to their owner/s. The *right* of a salvor to be rewarded for any such intervention was established long ago under common law but the *amount* of any such reward depends upon the facts and circumstances of each particular case. In the end, this may have to be decided by an arbitrator or, if necessary, the court – which, in these matters, is the Admiralty section of the High Court.

In practice, salvage operations of any magnitude are the subject of a contractual agreement between the parties concerned and it can be appreciated how the problems of the master of a ship in trouble can be magnified by delay due to the negotiation of a salvage contract by means of the ship's radio or by loud-hailers in a force-9 gale. A commonly used basis for such a contract is the standard form of salvage agreement issued by Lloyds; it embraces the principle: 'no cure – no pay' and provides for the amount of the salvor's reward, if not agreed by the parties, to be decided by an arbitrator appointed by the Committee of Lloyds from their panel of senior counsel who normally practice in the Admiralty section of the Queen's Bench division of the High Court. The Rules governing the Lloyds arbitration procedure provide for appeals on awards to be referred to a single appeal arbitrator, who is also a senior counsel, retained for that purpose.

10 Arbitration in Industrial Disputes

Trade Disputes

Although this book is mainly concerned with commercial arbitration, it would be incomplete without mentioning the role of arbitration in the settlement of disputes arising in industrial relations – i.e. 'trade disputes' – defined by the Trade Union and Labour Relations Act 1974 as disputes between employers and workers or between workers and workers in respect of one or more of the following matters

(a) the terms and conditions of employment (including physical conditions);
(b) the engagement/suspension/termination of employment and duties of employment;
(c) the demarcation of work/duties between workers;
(d) discipline;
(e) trade union membership;
(f) facilities for trade union officials;
(g) negotiating machinery related to the above matters.

It has long been recognised that relationships between 'employers' and 'employees' (or 'masters' and 'servants') are in a special category – mainly because disputes between such parties are not necessarily amenable to settlement by judicial pronouncements. The happiness and prosperity of human beings within their general working environment are so fundamental that any question or dispute which arises about such matters cannot be settled finally except *by agreement*. And even when such agreement appears to have been reached, there often remains a residual root-element of dissatisfaction which grows to produce future problems.

In the booklet entitled: *'Conciliation and Arbitration in Industrial Disputes'* (Heffer & Sons, 1952) J. R. W. Alexander wrote: '. . . commercial arbitration should be distinguished from conciliation and arbitration in industrial disputes. In fact, the two systems should be compared only with considerable caution, for in origin, purpose and procedure they are very different'. The distinction between the nature of trade disputes and those arising from other relationships was recognised in the Conciliation Act 1896 and the Industrial Court Act 1919. More recently, S.3(5) of the Employment Protection Act 1975 specifically excludes the application of Part I of the Arbitration Act 1950 to trade disputes under that Section. Instead, various arrangements designed for dealing with and settling trade disputes have been established by Statutes and/or Regulations specifically concerned with industrial relations. Furthermore, SS.13 and 14 of the Trade Union and Labour Relations Act 1974 provide that an act done by any person, trade union or employer's association in contemplation or furtherance of a trade dispute shall not be actionable in tort.

Industrial Dispute Procedure

Currently, the official agency responsible for assisting management and employees to avoid trade disputes and, when necessary, to settle them is the Advisory, Conciliation and Arbitration Service (ACAS) – set up under the provisions of S.1 of the Employment Protection Act 1975. This is directed by a Council consisting of a chairman and nine members – three nominated by the Confederation of British Industry, three by the Trades Union Congress and three independent members. The service is non-governmental and operates from headquarters in London and eight regional offices. It is charged with the following main functions

(a) advisory and information services to industry;
(b) improvement of collective bargaining;
(c) conciliation in industrial disputes;
(d) provision of arbitration services.

Parties requiring arbitration services under S.3 of the Employment Protection Act 1975 should apply to the appropriate regional office of ACAS or, when national issues are involved, to headquarters. If the matter then becomes the subject of arbitration proceedings, the parties bear their own costs but the fees/expenses of the arbitrator/s are paid by ACAS.

It is evident that arbitration in trade disputes is related to that of commercial arbitration in some matters of principle and general procedure but differs from it in other fundamental respects. For example, an essential pre-requisite before a trade dispute can be referred to arbitration is the agreement of all parties concerned to do so *after* a dispute has arisen although, in some circumstances, it may be possible to proceed with an arbitration upon the request of one party only – e.g. under S.98 of the Employment Protection Act.

Only then can ACAS refer the dispute to

(a) one or more persons specifically appointed by ACAS for that purpose, or;

(b) the Central Arbitration Committee (CAC) provided for in S.10 of the Employment Protection Act.

It is important to note that ACAS and CAC are independent bodies although, being concerned in the same sphere of interest, they inevitably work along parallel lines.

Implementation of Award

Because S.3(5) of the Employment Protection Act excludes the application of Part I of the 1950 to arbitrations in trade disputes, awards in such disputes are not *legally* binding but, in practice, it is found that the parties, having agreed to refer their dispute to arbitration, and thereby demonstrating their desire to reach a settlement by that means, have usually implemented the ensuing award. It is only in a relatively few cases that an award is not accepted and/or implemented by those concerned and this is why, inevitably, such cases become notorious – especially when they are followed by industrial actions. An example of this occurred when members of the National Union of Journalists withdrew their labour in August 1980 because their employer (the proprietors of *The Times* newspaper) failed to implement an award by an independent arbitrator with regard to their remuneration. The reason for so failing was said to be that the employer could not meet the award within the commercial viability of the newspaper but the NUJ argued that a point of principle was at stake. Eventually (and, it could be said, inevitably) the matter was resolved, albeit with subsequent commercial consequences, on the basis of further compromise. Another and more recent example has been publicised by the disruptive action taken in 1981 by certain members of the Civil Service in support of their contention that a previous award had not been honoured, in this case, by Her Majesty's Government.

ACAS and CAC Activities

According to their annual reports, cases were referred to arbitration by ACAS in recent years as follows:

		1979	*1980*	*1981*	*1982*
Referred to –	Single arbitrator	304	237	212	194
	Ad hoc board of arbitrators	44	34	27	26
	Central Arbitration Committee	11	10	5	10
	Post Office Arbitration Tribunal	3	7	1	–
		362	288	245	230

See Table 7 in ACAS Reports

Of these, the majority (75–85%) were concerned with subsidiary matters of terms and conditions of employment, some 10–15% dealt with dismissals and disciplinary matters and the remainder with demarcation, redundancy and other issues.

As will be seen from the following figures, the greater activity has been in the field of conciliation

	1979	*1980*	*1981*	*1982*
Cases in which a settlement was wholly or substantially achieved by conciliation	1786	1467	1364	1292
Unsuccessful results	498	443	352	342
Totals	2284	1910	1716	1634

See Table 1(b) in ACAS Reports

In the same years, references to the Central Arbitration Committee including those under Schedule 11 of the Employment Protection Act (claims that an employer is not observing the relevant terms and conditions of employment in his establishment) were as follows:

	1979	*1980*	*1981*	*1982*
Claims referred	341	323	65*	2
Claims settled/withdrawn	123	83	5*	2
Claims rejected	12	2	–	–
Outstanding	106	2	–	–

See Table 10 in ACAS Reports

*Schedule 11 was repealed in 1980.

Another sphere of activity by the CAC is the investigation of questions whether particular firms are observing the Fair Wages Resolution 1946 – adopted by the House of Commons on 14 October 1946 as a measure designed to ensure that government contractors pay fair wages and observe fair conditions of employment. It has no statutory force but its terms are incorporated in standard conditions of government contracts and, as such, are binding upon the contractors concerned.

Other Tribunals

A wide variety of other tribunals exist and operate under the provisions of such statutory enactments as the Industrial Tribunals (Labour Relations) Regulations 1974, the Sex Discrimination Act 1975, the Race Relations Act

1976; also, under the appeal procedure prescribed by the Employment Appeal Tribunals Rules 1976.

In Conclusion

The history of industrial relations in general as well as in particular industries are fields of study in their own right and the numerous publications in this field include those mentioned in the Bibliography. However, as a further point for discussion, it would avoid confusion and, perhaps, be more realistic to use some other term in place of 'arbitration' in trade disputes. For example, 'statutory negotiation' could be seen as a natural progression from first-stage conciliation by referring any matter/s not thereby resolved to a second-stage Board or Tribunal within an ACAS (or similar) framework. Then, whatever emerges as the 'findings' of such Board or Tribunal, it should not be referred to as an 'award'. Some other term such as 'ruling' or 'adjudication' could help to dispel the erroneous impression in some minds that arbitrator's awards in industrial disputes are as binding as they are in commercial disputes.

In this connection, it will be remembered, the dispute between the Water Council and ancillary workers in the water industry was settled in the early part of 1983 on the basis of adjudication by an *ad hoc* 'Committee of Enquiry' – after the trade unions concerned had refused to pre-commit their members to a 'binding arbitration' procedure. Semantics, it seems, can be also invoked as a face-saving element in such circumstances.

The common factors in commercial and industrial disputes are the endemic characteristics of human behaviour which, in general, seem to have remained as they were when Solon (circa 500 BC) declared: 'Men keep their engagements when it is to the advantage of both parties not to break them.' A twentieth-century cynic might feel like re-phrasing this: 'Men keep their engagements voluntarily as long as they feel it pays them to do so.' This seems to be true in all sorts of human relationships.

11 General Services and Special Schemes

General Advice and Services

The intention of contracting parties that any disputes arising out of their commercial activities are to be settled by arbitration should be written into the terms and conditions governing their trading relationships. Alternatively, such provisions can be incorporated in an *ad hoc* arbitration agreement made subsequently. It will probably save time and trouble at a later date if such provisions are extended to define how and by whom any appointment of the arbitrator/s shall be made and the rules by which any arbitration proceedings shall be governed. Furthermore, in international trading agreements, it is prudent to pre-agree and prescribe for certain other matters such as the law, the language and the locale related to any such proceedings. It is understandable, therefore, that some people who become involved in the agreement of such arbitration provisions or, at a later stage, in the initiation of arbitration proceedings may feel themselves to be at a disadvantage in not knowing how or where they can obtain any necessary advice or other assistance.

In general, their best move in such circumstances will be to consult a solicitor and/or to get in touch with the Chartered Institute of Arbitrators (CIArb). Members of professional bodies can usually get advice from the legal advisors of such bodies and 'consumers' can seek help from Citizens Advice Bureaux. Most professional/technical bodies and trade associations can supply the names of members who are able and willing to act as experts or arbitrators and, when so authorised by the parties, such bodies can also nominate an arbitrator to adjudicate in a particular dispute. Parties who are not pre-committed to accept an appointment by a particular third-party – and even when they are – can agree to have an arbitrator nominated by the CIArb and any such nomination can be made subject to any particular rules which the parties have agreed to adopt after, if necessary, discussing their particular wishes with the Institute.

Other possible ways of proceeding are to adopt and implement the rules of other bodies or the special schemes established for the settlement of particular sorts of dispute. For international commercial contracts, for example, the Rules of the International Chamber of Commerce (ICC) or those of the United Nations Commission on International Trade Law (UNCITRAL) can be adopted as the basis for any related arbitration proceedings.

Bodies from whom services and/or advice can be obtained are mentioned below.

Administered Arbitration

Arbitrations under the rules of a particular body or scheme are sometimes referred to as 'administered arbitrations' (or 'institutional arbitrations') when their general administration is handled, as provided by such rules, by an 'administering authority' – being the Institute, Court, Trade Association or other Body so nominated. As such, administered arbitrations fall into the general category of arbitrations in which the arbitrator is supported by an administration service which leaves him fully in control of the proceedings as a whole but relieves him of the 'clerical mechanics' which he would otherwise have to perform himself. In such cases the respective roles and responsibilities of the arbitrator and the administering body need to be defined in the relative rules and carefully observed.

At the same time, there is no reason why any arbitrator, by whomsoever appointed, should not (by agreement of the parties) avail himself of any such administrative services provided he does not thereby abdicate from any of his basic responsibilities. In fact, arbitrators with limited experience may be well advised to use such a service at least until they have acquired a greater degree of confidence and, even after that, they may wish to continue to do so for various reasons. The reasonable cost of such services may be recovered as part of the arbitrator's expenses in connection with the arbitration.

Some Organisations Concerned with Arbitration

The Law Society
113 Chancery Lane
London WC2A 1PL 01 242 1222

Chartered Institute of Arbitrators (CIArb)
75 Cannon Street
London EC4N 5BH 01 236 8761/2

London Court of International Arbitration (LCIA)
(Administered by CIArb)

International Chamber of Commerce (ICC)

Headquarters	38 Cours Albert l'er 75008 PARIS	359 05 92
British National Committee	6–14 Dean Farrar Street London SW1H 0DT	01 222 3755/7

London Maritime Arbitration Association (LMAA)
The Baltic Exchange
14–20 St. Mary Axe
London EC3

Advisory, Conciliation and Arbitration Service (ACAS)
11–12 St. James's Square
London SW1Y 4LA 01 214 6000

Central Arbitration Committee (CAC)
1 The Abbey Garden
Great College Street
London SW1

Office of Fair Trading (OFT)
Chancery House
53 Chancery Lane
London WC2A 1SP 01 242 2858

Consumers' Association (CA)
14 Buckingham Street
London WC2N 6DS 01 839 1222

Citizens' Advice Bureaux (CAB)

Headquarters	26 Bedford Square London WC1B 3HU	01 636 4066
Locally	See local telephone directories	

Professional Bodies
Most UK professional societies/institutes are active in their particular fields – see appropriate publications for details.

Trade Associations
See appropriate Trade Directories for details.

London Chamber of Commerce and Industry (LCCI)
69 Cannon Street
London EC4N 5AB 01 248 4444
Other places – see local directories

Local Authorities
Consumer Protection Departments
(See local telephone directories)

Some Special Schemes

The following organisations are among those for whom the CIArb operates a subsidised but independent arbitration scheme for the settlement of disputes which cannot be resolved by direct negotiation between members of those associations and their respective customers:

The Association of British Travel Agents (ABTA)
53–54 Newman Street
London W1P 4AH 01 580 8281

The Motor Agents' Association (MAA)
201 Great Portland Street
London W1 01 580 9122

National House-Building Council (NH-BC)
Conciliation Division
Hill House
Hill Avenue
Amersham HP6 5BJ 02403 3958/9

The Electricity Council
Marketing Department
Trafalgar Buildings
1 Charing Cross
London SW1A 2BS 01 930 6757

The Association of Manufacturers of Domestic Electrical Appliances (AMDEA)
8 Leicester Street
London WC2H 7BN 01 437 0678

Society of Motor Manufacturers and Traders (SMMT)
Forbes House
Halkin Street
London SW1X 7DS 01 235 7000

Scottish Motor Traders' Association (SMTA)
3 Palmerston Place,
Edinburgh EH12 5AQ 031 225 3643

In addition, most of the major oil companies have set up special arbitration schemes for resolving disputes arising out of agreements with their filling-station concessionaires. Similar schemes are operated by the CIArb for the settlement of disputes between their customers and certain independent travel agents, the Post Office, the National Caravan Council, the Vehicle Builders and Repairers Association as well as other associations representing funeral services, mail order services, the furniture industry and the photographic industry.

Arbitration schemes are also operated by certain trade associations for the resolution of disputes between their members. Such schemes are normally subject to the provisions of the Arbitration Acts and they are also governed by particular rules adopted within the flexibility permitted by those Acts. One of the most comprehensive and extensive schemes of this sort is the one operated by the Grain and Feed Trade Association (GAFTA).

Readers interested in the field of counselling can obtain information about services available in a wide variety of circumstances from:

British Association for Counselling (BAC)
26 Bedford Square
London WC1B 3HU 01 436 4066

12 A Backward Look

Having reached this point it is worth pausing to look back and thus be reminded of how things have become what they are today. In doing so, it becomes evident that while the *style* of human relationships has changed considerably in all sections of society, the nature of human behaviour has changed very little – if at all. Human relationships are often affected by misunderstandings which may lead to disputes, aggression and other disruptive behaviour. No section of society is immune; it has always been part of the social scene.

Social Conventions

Inter-tribal or personal quarrels in primitive societies were (and, in some places, still are) settled promptly and sometimes violently by direct action. The result may not always have been 'fair' because, irrespective of the merits of the case, the stronger contestant will usually defeat the weaker. Today, in so-called advanced societies, we have abandoned the tomahawk, club and poisoned arrow; instead, we use other weapons such as demonstrations, working-to-rule, strikes, 'sending to Coventry' or sacking those who do not conform, character assassination and other such unhappy features of modern life. Thus, metaphorically speaking, the use of knives is still in vogue and the fact that they are operated with clinical efficiency in sterile conditions makes them even more effective as a means of achieving what would otherwise be impossible.

To return to the natural development of primitive societies, one can imagine how, in order to avoid violence or injustice, the tribal chief and/or village elders would listen to problems and quarrels and help to sort them out within the framework of the accepted social pattern. This process would have been shaped and developed progressively by one generation after another so that, in the process, people became aware of what was and what was not acceptable in their society. The principle of 'trial-by-peers' ('equals') was a further development – to be seen, for example, in the proceedings of the UK

Parliament when erring members of the House of Lords stood for trial by their peers under their rights established by Magna Carta and maintained until the Criminal Justice Act 1948 abolished them.

The same principle underlies the system of trial-by-jury, whereby questions of fact in criminal cases are decided by a jury composed of twelve ordinary citizens. They listen to the allegations as presented in court, and weigh up the conflicting submissions made by the prosecution and defence; they then have to agree and declare their verdict but without giving reasons for coming to their decision.

The Emergence of Arbitration

In effect, therefore, arbitration has emerged as an acceptable way of resolving disputes by the application of the rules of natural justice within the law. By this means, a third party helps the disputing parties by sorting out their differences – provided that they have agreed in advance to accept his decision.

The futility of a third party's attempt to intervene in a dispute without such agreement is illustrated by the Old Testament story of what happened when Moses came upon an Egyptian and an Israelite fighting each other. Moses tried to settle the quarrel without having been invited or authorised to do so, and obviously without any agreement by the parties that they would accept his 'decision'. The immediate result of his intervention was that the Egyptian lay dead while the Israelite returned to his base but, in due course, Moses was accused of murder and had to flee.

Another Old Testament story illustrates the operation of a recognised arbitration process. In this case, two women each claimed the same child as her own and went to King Solomon to ask him to resolve the problem. Having heard the women, Solomon suggested that the baby be cut into two so that each could have one half. Thereupon, one woman immediately gave up her claim but, by her so doing, Solomon recognised in her the real mother and awarded her the baby. Thus, the term 'judgment of Solomon' has come to mean 'split the difference'.

In the Middle Ages (13th to 16th centuries) disputes arising from transactions between traders were often settled by a 'law merchant' – a sort of mobile arbitrator who, like his clients, travelled from place to place to offer his services at a regular cycle of fairs and markets.

This custom was found, for example, in Mediterranean cities, especially in Italy; in England, it became the function of what was known as 'the Piepowder Court' – a corruption of the colloquial term *Pieds Poudrés* ('dusty feet') applied with direct and obvious significance to the travelling law-merchant – as further described in *Little Red Book of Bristol,* compiled at the instigation of the then Recorder of Bristol who 'caused the ordinances, customs and liberties . . . together with certain laws, other memoranda, and divers necessary things to be inviolably kept in perpetual remembrance' from 1344 to 1574 to be thus recorded. A supplementary publication was *'Great Red Book of Bristol'* containing similar records related to the 14th, 15th and 16th centuries.

The Ouzel Galley

An interesting and relevant digression is found in a story which began in 1695 when certain Irish merchants, finding themselves isolated from their customary trading with the English mainland, commissioned a ship, the *Ouzel*, for a trading mission to the Eastern Mediterranean. She was a galley, a sturdy vessel of about 80 tons displacement with a crew of 37 and armed with brass cannons. Nothing was heard of the ship after she had sailed for five years and, in the meantime, the insurers paid up on the assumption that she had become a total loss. Then, in 1700, she arrived back in Dublin harbour with a remarkable story. She had suffered various misfortunes on her way and then had been captured by North African pirates, who made her crew prisoners. Eventually, the crew recaptured the ship and sailed back to Ireland with the pirate's loot still on board. However, her arrival created problems regarding both her ownership and that of the cargo which developed into a long-drawn-out legal argument with little apparent prospect of solution.

After a further period of five years, it was agreed that the legal arguments should be abandoned and that the proceeds from the sale of the ship and her cargo should be used to set up a fund to establish (in 1705) the Ouzel Galley Society 'For the Arbitration of all disputes to them referred relating to Trade and Commerce, the expenses whereof are apportioned to the benefit of decayed merchants.' Later, the Society was absorbed into the Dublin Chamber of Commerce.

Dr. Barnardo's Homes

A much later example of early arbitration proceedings occurred in connection with the admirable institution known to all as Dr Barnardo's. The motive and methods of the founder were at one stage attacked by critics in such serious terms that the work seemed likely to suffer and Dr Barnardo was eventually persuaded to agree to refer the accusation to arbitration. Accordingly, an Arbitration Board was established under a Rule made on 7 June 1877 by the High Court (Exchequer Division), under the Common Law Procedure Act 1854. Members of the Board were – John Maule QC, Recorder of Leeds, Canon John Miller DD, Vicar of Rochester and William Graham, Ex-MP (Liberal) for Glasgow. They heard the case at a hearing which lasted thirty-eight days at the Great George Street headquarters of what is now the Royal

Institution of Chartered Surveyors. As part of the proceedings they visited each of the bases from which Dr Barnardo's work was conducted, and received reports from independent experts on the accounts and administrative arrangements. Their Award, published on 15 October 1877 and commented on by *The Times* and other newspapers on 19 and 20 October 1877, was not a total commendation of Dr Barnardo's conduct of the work or of himself at the hearing. However, with regard to the substance of the accusations against him, the Award declared that they were not justified, adding that the work continued to be worthy of public confidence and support. In conclusion, the Board expressed the earnest hope that the Award would be accepted as final and that all defamatory charges would immediately cease. Twelve years later, the Arbitration Act of 1889 could have made the first part of that plea unnecessary.

An Ecclesiastical Problem

More recently, in 1973, a different sort of dispute was also settled by arbitration, an account of which appeared in *Arbitration* (October 1973). Two church congregations in Scotland had agreed to merge but could not agree about which of their existing premises should be used thereafter. Since the dispute was in Scotland, the matter was referred to three Arbiters who, after hearing representations by all concerned and carefully inspecting the two sets of buildings and their equipment, announced their findings. These included a decision about which of the premises were to be used, and an expression of sympathy with those who would be disappointed by their decision – which, they also hoped, would be accepted as having been made carefully and responsibly for the good of the Christian cause in the locality.

And finally . . .

The lessons of history as well as current observations confirm that, fundamentally, human behaviour is regulated by social rather than legal constraints. As Lord Scarman said in his Alexander Lecture (1975); 'The whole structure of law hangs on the slender thread of public consent.'

By mutual consent, therefore, parties to a commercial transaction should expend as much time, effort and expense as is necessary to pre-empt the possibility of future misunderstanding about their respective intentions – thus following the long-established principle: Prevention is better than cure.

And, what is more, the erection of a fence at the top of a cliff is a better use of resources than the operation of a casualty clearing centre at its foot!

PART II
A LAYMAN'S GUIDE TO THE ARBITRATION ACTS

The 1950 Act

Introduction

A For authoritative information, reference should be made to the official text of the Arbitration Act 1950 – referred to as 'this Act' in this part of the Guide.

B The purpose of this Act was to consolidate the Arbitration Acts 1889–1934.

C Certain amendments to the 1950 Act as made by the 1975 and the 1979 Acts are mentioned where applicable in each section of this chapter.

D The qualification: 'Unless a contrary intention is expressed *(in the arbitration agreement)*' in SS.1–6–8(1)–8(2)–9–12(1)–12(2)–12(3)–14–15–16–17–18(1) should be particularly noted because, to avoid constant repetition, the sections to which this qualifying phrase can apply are related to this Note in the Guide which follows. This provision allows considerable flexibility for the parties to agree the procedure whereby their disputes are to be settled.

E Subject to the context, the term 'arbitrator' in the text includes 'umpire'; the term 'the court' in this Act means the High Court or a High Court judge.

F S.6 of the 1975 Act provides, in effect, that nothing in that Act affects the right of a party other than under that Act and Part II of the 1950 Act.

G S.7(1) of the 1979 Act stipulates that the provisions of SS.1–6 of that Act are deemed to be incorporated in the following provisions of this Act:
S.14: interim awards,
S.28: terms as to costs of orders,
S.30: Crown to be bound,
S.31: application to statutory arbitrations,
S.32: meaning of 'Arbitration agreement'.

H S.15(6) of the Administration of Justice Act 1982 inserts new Section 19A in this Act.

I The application of the foregoing provisions is also indicated by the notes/comments in italics which appear in particular Sections of the Guide.

Part I General provisions

S.1 Authority of arbitrators and umpires to be irrevocable

Once appointed, no arbitrator can be removed except by leave of the High Court. *(See Note (D) above.)*

S.2 Death of a party (1)–(3)

Neither the arbitration agreement nor the arbitrator's appointment nor a party's right of action is extinguished by the death of a party.

S.3 Bankruptcy (1)–(2)

An arbitration clause in any contract to which one of the parties becomes bankrupt remains effective if the trustee in bankruptcy adopts the contract.

S.4 Staying court proceedings where there is a submission to arbitration

Arbitration can take precedence over litigation when the disputing parties are bound by an arbitration agreement. Accordingly, any related court proceedings may be stayed on application by a party before he condones such proceedings and provided that the court is satisfied that there is no good reason why the matter should not proceed to arbitration.

(i) *This provision is extended by S.1(2) of the 1975 Act in relation to non-domestic arbitration agreements.*
(ii) *S.4(2) is deleted by S.8(2) of the 1975 Act*

S.5 Reference of interpleader issues to arbitration

Interpleader proceedings can be stayed in favour of arbitration when an arbitration agreement exists between the parties concerned.

S.6 When reference is to a single arbitrator

Unless otherwise provided, every arbitration agreement is deemed to provide for a reference to a single arbitrator. *(See Note (D) above).*

S.7 Power of parties in certain cases to supply vacancy

Subject to the High Court's power to intervene, provision is made for:

(a) replacement of an arbitrator who refuses to act or becomes incapable of acting as such;
(b) proceeding in default by a party in appointing one of two arbitrators.

S.8 Umpires

(1) When two arbitrators are appointed they must appoint an umpire. *(See Note (D) above.)*

(2)–(3) When two arbitrators have failed to agree or the High Court so orders, the umpire must act as sole arbitrator.

(i) *S.6(1) of the 1979 Act provides that the appointment of an umpire may be at any time before the two arbitrators fail to agree – and must be made immediately upon their so failing.*
(ii) *See Note (D) above.*

S.9 Agreements for reference to three arbitrators

(i) *This section is deleted by S.6(2) of the 1979 Act.*
(ii) *In its place a new section restores the provision that an award by any two of three arbitrators is binding.*
(iii) *See Note (D) above.*

S.10 Power of court in certain cases to appoint an arbitrator or umpire

Appointments may be made by the High Court when:

(a) the parties cannot concur in the appointment of a single arbitrator;
(b) an appointed arbitrator refuses to act or becomes incapable of acting;
(c) the parties or two arbitrators fail to appoint an umpire or third arbitrator when so required.

(i) *Paragraph (c) is amended by S.6(3) of the 1979 Act but without materially affecting its substance. (See also S.8(3) thereof)*

(ii) *S.6(4) of the 1979 Act provides that new Clause 10(2) is deemed to have been inserted in this Act. This prescribes the procedure to be followed when a third party nominated as the appointing authority fails to act.*

S.11 Reference to official referee

If the arbitration agreement so provides, an Official Referee must hear and determine the case, subject to any order of the High Court.

(i) *The title and functions of Official Referees were merged into those of Commercial Court judges under the provisions of SS.3 and 4 of the Administration of Justice Act 1970.*
(ii) *Schedule 3 of the Administration of Justice Act 1970 is amended by S.8(3)(c) of the 1979 act.*
(iii) *See also S.5(3)–(6) of the 1979 Act.*

S.12 Conduct of proceedings, witnesses, etc.

(1) An arbitrator has the power to examine the parties and all others claiming through them and to inspect documents and all things otherwise necessary. *(See Note (D) above.)*

(2)–(3) Such examination may be on oath or affirmation. *(See Note (D) above.)*

(4) Any party may issue a writ of *subpoena ad testificandum* or *subpoena duces tecum* subject as stipulated.

(5) The High Court may order the issue of a writ of *habeas corpus ad testificandum* to bring a prisoner before an arbitrator.

(6) The High Court may make the same orders in respect of arbitration proceedings as could be made in court proceedings with regard to certain matters (see below), without prejudice to the arbitrator's powers in respect thereof under the arbitration agreement or otherwise. These matters are:

(a) security for costs,
(b) discovery of documents and interrogatories,
(c) evidence by affidavit,
(d) evidence on commission,
(e) location, custody or disposal of goods in question,
(f) securing the amount in dispute,
(g) obtaining and preserving real evidence,
(h) interim injunctions; appointment of receiver.

S.13 Time for making award

(1) There is no limit to the period within which an award must be issued unless the arbitration agreement so provides or an award is remitted by the High Court. *(See also S.22(2).)*

(2) Any such time limit imposed by this Act or the arbitration agreement can be extended by the High Court before or after such time has expired.

(3) Upon application, the High Court may remove an arbitrator who is unreasonably slow in entering upon or proceeding with the reference or publishing his award; if so removed, an arbitrator is not entitled to any fees. 'Proceeding with the reference' includes, when two arbitrators fail to agree, giving notice of such failure to the parties and to the umpire.

S.14 Interim awards

Interim awards can be made. They are subject to the general provisions in this Act in respect of awards. *(See Notes (D) and (G) above.)*

S.15 Specific performance

Arbitrators have the same power as the High Court to order specific performance of any contract except one related to land. *(See Note (D) above.)*

S.16 Awards to be final

Arbitrators' awards are final and binding upon the parties and any persons claiming under them. *(See Note (D) above.)*

S.17 Power to correct slips

Arbitrators have power to correct clerical mistakes or errors in their awards arising from accidental slips or omissions. *(See Note (D) above and also S.18(4) in respect of costs.)*

S.18 Costs

(1) An arbitrator has full discretion to tax and settle costs and to decide how costs shall be assessed and by whom and to whom and how such costs shall be paid. *(See Note (D) above.)*

(2) Unless the award otherwise directs costs are taxable in the High Court.

(3) Any provision in an arbitration agreement whereby the parties or either of them agree to pay their own costs in any event is void unless such agreement is made after the relative dispute has arisen.

(4) If no provision is made in an award with regard to costs, either party can apply to the arbitrator within 14 days (or longer if the High Court allows) for an order to supply the necessary directions; then, after hearing any party who wishes to be heard, the arbitrator must amend his award by including such directions as he thinks fit.

(5) The High Court may in respect of arbitration proceedings charge property recovered or preserved in the proceedings as security for solicitors' costs under S.69 of the Solicitors' Act 1932.

S.19 Taxation of arbitrator's or umpire's fees

(1) Should an arbitrator refuse to deliver his award until his fees are paid, the High Court may on application order that such fees are paid into court and the award issued thereupon. Such fees are then taxable in the High Court and the amount

found to be properly chargeable by the arbitrator is passed on to him while the balance, if any, is returned to the applicant.

(2) Such application can be made by either party but not if the arbitrator's fees have been agreed in advance.

(3)–(4) Any taxation of fees is subject to review and the arbitrator is entitled to be heard on any such taxation or review.

S.19A Power of arbitrator to award interest

New Section inserted by S.15(6) of the Administration of Justice Act 1982

(1) Unless a contrary provision is expressed therein, every arbitration agreement is deemed to provide that an arbitrator (or umpire) may award simple interest at the rate and for the period he thinks fit on:

(a) any sum included in the reference and paid before the relative award is made; and,
(b) any sum included in such award but not for any period after the date thereof.

(2) The power conferred by (1) above is without prejudice to any other power of an arbitrator (or umpire) to award interest.

S.20 Interest on awards

Unless the award otherwise directs, interest is payable from the date of the award at the same date as a judgment debt on the amount directed to be paid by the award.

S.21 Statement of case

This section is repealed by S.1 of the 1979 Act.

S.22 Power to remit award

(1) The High Court may remit to the arbitrator the matters referred or any part of them for his reconsideration.

(2) If so, and unless otherwise directed, the arbitrator must make his amended award within three months of the date of the order.

S.23 Removal of arbitrator and setting aside of award

(1) The High Court may remove an arbitrator who misconducts himself or the proceedings.

(2) If so, or if an award is procured improperly, the High Court may set aside the award.

(3) On application to have an award set aside the High Court may order that any money payable as provided in the award shall be paid into court or otherwise secured.

S.24 Power of court to give relief where arbitrator is not impartial or the dispute involves questions of fraud

(1) The court cannot refuse a post-dispute application

(a) to remove the arbitrator named or designated in a pre-dispute arbitration agreement, or,
(b) to restrain a party or the arbitrator from proceeding

solely on the ground that the arbitrator's potential incapability of being impartial was or could have been known by the applicant when the agreement was made.

(2) If a dispute otherwise referrable to arbitration involves an allegation of fraud, the High Court may set aside the arbitration agreement and allow the arbitrator's authority to be revoked.

(3) In such circumstances the High Court may refuse to stay court proceedings brought in breach of the arbitration agreement.

S.3(3) of the 1979 Act limits the powers of the High Court under S.24(2) of this Act in respect of certain disputes having a foreign element.

S.25 Power of court where arbitrator is removed or authority of arbitrator is revoked

(1) On application the High Court may fill vacancies unless a single arbitrator or all of a greater number have been removed by the Court.

(2) If the sole or all of a greater number of arbitrators are so removed, the High Court may either appoint a sole arbitrator to act in place of the one or more removed or set aside the arbitration agreement in respect of the dispute referred.

(3) A person so appointed by the High Court has the same powers as if he had been appointed under the relative arbitration agreement.

(4) If the High Court sets aside an arbitration agreement, it may also set aside any provision it contains that the making of an award shall precede any action with respect to any matter to which the agreement applies.

S.26 Enforcement of award

An award may, by leave of the High Court, be enforced as would a judgment of the High Court.

S.27 Power of court to extend time for commencing of arbitration proceedings

The High Court may, in certain circumstances, extend the time within which arbitration proceedings must be initiated to comply with the terms of an arbitration agreement.

S.28 Terms as to costs

The authority making any order under Part I of this Act has discretion to make an order as to costs. *(See Note (G) above.)*

The proviso referring to S.4(2) of this Act is deleted by S.8(2)(b) of the 1975 Act.

S.29 Extension of S.496 of the Merchant Shipping Act 1894

(1)–(3) 'Legal proceedings' in S.496(3) of the Merchant Shipping Act 1894 includes arbitration.

S.30 Crown to be bound

Part I of this Act applies to any dispute involving the Crown, the Duchy of Lancaster or the Duchy of Cornwall. *(See Note (G) above.)*

The proviso referring to S.4(2) of this Act is deleted by S.8(2)(c) of the 1975 Act.

S.31 Application of Part I to statutory arbitrations

(1) Subject as provided, Part I of this Act applies to every arbitration under any other act; *i.e. to statutory arbitrations.*

(2) The following provisions of this Act do not apply to statutory arbitrations:

S.2(1) : Death of a party.
S.3 : Bankruptcy.
S.5 : Interpleader proceedings.
S.18(3) : Costs.
S.24 : Power of High Court to give relief.
S.25 : Power of High Court when arbitrator removed.
S.27 : Power of High Court to extend time.
S.29 : Extension of Merchant Shipping Act 1894.

(i) *The proviso referring to S.4(2) of this Act is deleted by S.8(2)(d) of the 1975 Act.*
(ii) *See Note (G) above.*
(iii) *S.7(3) of the 1979 Act stipulates that the provisions of this section with reference to statutory arbitrations do not apply to arbitrations under S.92 of the County Courts Act 1959.*

S.32 Meaning of 'arbitration agreement'

A written agreement to submit present or future differences to arbitration, whether an arbitrator is named therein or not.

(i) *See Note (G) above.*
(ii) *See S.7 of the 1979 Act.*

S.33 Operation of Part I

Part I of this Act does not apply to arbitration proceedings commenced before this Act comes into effect. It applies to proceedings commenced thereafter irrespective of the date of the relative arbitration agreement.

S.34 Extent of Part I

This Section is amended by S.8(2)(e) of the 1975 Act to read: 'None of the provisions of this Part of the Act shall extend to Scotland or Northern Ireland.'

Part II Enforcement of certain foreign awards

S.35 Awards to which Part II applies

(1) Subject to S.2 of the 1975 Act, Part II applies to any award made after 28 July 1924

> in pursuance of an arbitration agreement related to the Protocol set out in the First Schedule (i.e. the 1923 League of Nations Protocol) and, between persons of whom one is subject to the jurisdiction of one of the powers who are parties to the Convention set out in the Second Schedule (i.e. the 1927 Geneva Convention) and the other is subject to the jurisdiction of another such power,

in one of the territories to which the said Convention applies. An award to which Part II applies is a 'foreign award'.

(2)–(3) Sundry provisions with regard to Orders in Council.

S.2 of the 1975 Act excludes the application of Part II of this Act to any Convention award which would otherwise be a foreign award.

S.36 Effect of foreign awards

A foreign award, subject as provided in Part II, is enforceable equally as an arbitrator's award under S.26 of this Act.

S.37 Conditions for enforcement of foreign awards

(1) To be enforceable, a foreign award must satisfy certain stipulated criteria.

(2) A foreign award cannot be enforced if it has been annulled in the country in which it was made or if the party against whom enforcement is sought is disadvantaged or if the award is defective by omission of matters referred or inclusion of matters not referred.

(3) The High Court may defer or refuse an order to enforce a foreign award when,

prima facie, there are adequate grounds on which an application for annulment may be made to the competent tribunal.

S.38 Evidence

(1) An application to enforce a foreign award must be supported by the original or certified copy of the award and evidence that it has become final; also such other evidence as necessary to prove that the award is a foreign award and satisfies the stipulations in S.37(1)(a)–(b)–(c) of this Act.

(2) A certified translation into English of any such documentary evidence must be produced by the party seeking enforcement. This certification must be by a diplomatic or consular agent of the country to which such party belongs.

(3) Further rules with respect to evidence may be made by the High Court under S.99 of the Supreme Court of Judicature (Consolidation) Act 1925.

S.39 Meaning of 'final award'

An award is not final if proceedings to contest its validity are pending.

S.40 Saving for other rights, etc.

(a) Part II does not affect the rights of any person to enforce in England the benefits of any award which such person would have if the said Part II or Part I of the Arbitration (Foreign Awards) Act 1930 had not been enacted.
(b) Part II does not apply to any award made under an arbitration agreement governed by English law.

S.41 Application of Part II to Scotland

Subject to certain amendments, as detailed, Part II applies to Scotland.

S.42 Application of Part II to Northern Ireland

Subject to certain amendments, as detailed, Part II applies to Northern Ireland.

S.43 Saving for pending proceedings

Any proceedings under Part I of the Arbitration (Foreign Awards) Act 1930, current at the commencement of this Act, may be continued under Part II as if initiated thereunder.

Part III General

S.44 Short title, commencement and repeal

(1) This Act is the Arbitration Act 1950.

(2) It came into operation on 1 September 1950.

(3) Certain existing legislation, as detailed, is repealed, including the Arbitration Acts 1889 and 1934.

First schedule

This sets out the text of the 1923 League of Nations Protocol in relation to S.35 in Part II.

Second schedule

This sets out the text of the 1927 Geneva Convention in relation to S.35 in Part II.

Statutes referred to

A Table of Statutes referred to in this Act is appended to this Act.

The 1975 Act

Introduction

A For authoritative information, reference should be made to the official text of the Arbitration Act 1975 – referred to in this part of the Guide as 'this Act'.

B The purpose of this Act is to give effect in the UK to the 1958 New York Convention on the Recognition and Enforcement of Foreign Arbitral Awards – generally referred to as the 'New York Convention'.

C This Act came into operation on 23 December 1975. On or about that date 18 States had ratified the Convention and 30 others, including the UK, had become parties by accession.

D The application of the foregoing provisions is also indicated by the notes/comments in italics which appear in particular Sections of the Guide.

S.1 Staying court proceedings where party proves arbitration agreement

(1) Parties and persons claiming under them can apply for a stay of court proceedings on the ground that a valid arbitration agreement exists between the parties in respect of the matters in dispute.

(2) This section applies to any arbitration agreement other than a domestic arbitration agreement. *(See (4) below.)* S.4(1) of the 1937 (Northern Ireland) Act does not apply to any arbitration agreement to which this section applies.

(3) In its application to Scotland, this Section is deemed to be amended to read 'sisting' instead of 'staying'.

(4) The term 'domestic arbitration agreement' in this Section is defined as an arbitration agreement which does not provide for arbitration in a State other than the UK and to which neither party is a national of or based in a state other than the UK at the time any proceedings are commenced.

S.2 Replacement of former provisions

SS.3–6 of this Act apply to the enforcement of awards under the 1958 New York Convention. Part II of the 1950 Act is excluded from applying to any Convention award which would otherwise be a foreign award.

S.3 Effect of Convention awards

(1) Convention awards are enforceable in England and Wales in the same manner as awards in respect of domestic arbitration agreements under S.26 of the 1950 Act. Provisions are also made for the enforcement of Convention awards in Scotland and Northern Ireland.

(2) Any Convention award enforceable under this Act is binding and may be relied upon as such in subsequent legal proceedings in the UK.

S.4 Evidence

The party seeking to enforce a Convention award must produce the original award (or a certified copy), the original arbitration agreement (or a certified copy), and a certified translation of either if the original is in a foreign language.

S.5 Refusal of enforcement

(1) Enforcement of a Convention award cannot be refused except in the circumstances stated.

(2) Subject as provided, enforcement of a Convention award may be refused by the High Court upon proof of incapacity, irregularity or inconclusiveness in the arbitration agreement, the parties, the proceedings or the award.

(3) Such refusal may be also given if the award purports to deal with a matter not capable of settlement by arbitration or if enforcement would be against public policy.

(4) Decisions in a Convention award about matters not referred can be ignored without affecting the validity of such award in respect of the matter/s referred.

(5) The High Court may order the adjournment of enforcement proceedings pending

the result of an application by a party to the competent authority for the annulment of an award; in so doing, the High Court may order the applicant for such annulment to provide security.

S.6 Saving

Nothing in this Act affects the rights of any party other than under this Act or Part II of the 1950 Act.

S.7 Interpretation

(1) In this Act:
'Arbitration agreement' means an agreement in writing (including letters/telegrams) to submit present or future differences to arbitration. 'Convention award' means a valid award made in a State other than the UK which is a party to the New York Convention. 'The New York Convention' means the Convention for the recognition and enforcement of foreign arbitral awards adopted on 10 June 1958 at the United Nations Conference in New York.

(2) The mention of a particular state in the relevant Order/s in Council is conclusive evidence that such state is a party to the New York Convention.

S.8 Short title, repeals, commencement and extent

(1) This Act may be referred to as the Arbitration Act 1975.

(2) Certain amendments (detailed) are made to the 1950 Act; these are noted in the relevant parts of this guide.

(3) This Act becomes effective on a date to be ordered by the Secretary of State. *(See Note (C) above.)*

(4) This Act specifically extends to Northern Ireland.

The 1979 Act

Introduction

A For authoritative information, reference should be made to the official text of the Arbitration Act 1979 – referred to in this part of the Guide as 'this Act'.

B The purpose of this Act is to amend the law relating to arbitrations and related matters.

C The effects of this Act on the 1950 and the 1975 Arbitration Acts are noted in the Guide to the relevant Sections thereof.

D This Act came into effect on 1 August 1979 subject to the proviso that it shall not apply to arbitration proceedings commenced before that date unless the parties so agree.

E SS.1 and 2 of this Act are amended by S.148 of the Supreme Court Act 1981.

F The application of the foregoing provisions is also indicated by the notes/comments in italics which appear in particular Sections of the Guide.

S.1 Judicial review of arbitration awards

(1) The Arbitration Act 1950 is referred to throughout as 'the principal Act'. S.21 of the principal Act ceases to have effect and, subject to (2) below, the High Court will not have power to remit an award on the ground of errors of fact or law in its contents.

(2) Subject to (3) below, appeals may be made to the High Court on any question of law arising out of an award; in response, the High Court may make an order to –

(a) confirm, vary or set aside the award, or

(b) remit the award for reconsideration of the arbitrator/umpire together with the court's findings on any point of law raised in the appeal. Unless otherwise ordered, the arbitrator/umpire to whom an award is thus remitted shall make his award within three months.

S.1 Judicial review of arbitration awards *(continued)*

(3) Appeals under (2) above may be brought by any party

(a) by consent of the other party, or
(b) by leave of the High Court subject to S.3.

(4) The High Court shall not grant leave under (3)(b) above unless the question raised could substantially affect the rights of a party and any such leave may be made subject to appropriate conditions.

(5) If, upon application under (3) above, it appears to the High Court that the award fails (adequately or totally) to set out the reasons for the award, the High Court may order the arbitrator or umpire to state such reasons as may be relevant in such detail as may be necessary to enable it to consider any question of law raised in such appeal.

(6) In cases where awards are made without stating the reasons, no order shall be made by the High Court under (5) above unless it is satisfied that

(a) one of the parties gave notice to the arbitrator or umpire before the award was issued that a reasoned award would be required, or
(b) there is some special reason why such notice was not given.

A new subsection is inserted by S.148(2) of the Supreme Court Act 1981 as follows:

(6A) Unless the High Court gives leave, no appeal shall lie to the Court of Appeal from a decision of the High Court

(a) to grant or refuse leave under subsection 3(b) or 5(b) above; or
(b) to make or not to make an order under subsection 5 above.

(7) No appeal from a decision of the High

Court in respect of an appeal under this section is permitted unless

(a) the High Court or the Court of Appeal gives leave, or
(b) it is certified by the High Court that a question of law related to its decision is of general importance or otherwise merits consideration by the Court of Appeal.

(8) An award which has been varied by the High Court has effect as if it were the award of the arbitrator/umpire.

S.2 Determination of preliminary point of law

(1) Upon application by any party and subject to (2) below and S.3, the High Court has power to determine a question of law arising in the course of a reference provided such application has the consent of

(a) the arbitrator/umpire who has entered on the reference, or
(b) all the other parties.

(2) The High Court cannot consider an application under (1)(a) above unless it is satisfied that

(a) the determination of the question raised could result in substantial savings in costs to the parties, and
(b) the question is such as would merit leave to appeal under S.1(3)(b).

A new subsection is inserted by S.148(3) of the Supreme Court Act 1981 as follows:

(2A) Unless the High Court gives leave, no appeal shall lie to the Court of Appeal from a decision of the High Court to entertain or not to entertain an application under subsection 1(a) above.

A corresponding amendment is made to subsection (3).

(3) The decision of the High Court under

subsection (1) above is a judgment within the meaning of S.27 of the Supreme Court of Judicature (Consolidation) Act 1925 (appeals to the Court of Appeal) but no appeal from such a decision is permitted save in the circumstances defined in S.1(7).

S.3 Exclusion agreements affecting rights under S.1 and S.2
(continued)

(1) Subject as follows in this section and in S.4 if the parties have entered into an agreement in writing (i.e. an exclusion agreement) to exclude the right of appeal under S.1 and S.2

(a) no leave to appeal may be granted by the High Court under S.1(3)(b),
(b) no leave to make an application with respect to an award can be granted by the High Court under S.1(5)(b),
(c) no application can be made by an arbitrator/umpire in respect of a question of law under S.2(1)(a).

(2) An exclusion agreement may be related to a particular award or awards under a particular reference or any other description of awards whether or not arising from the same reference; such agreement may be an exclusion agreement whether or not it is entered into before the passing of this Act and whether or not it forms part of an arbitration agreement.

(3) When

(a) a non-domestic arbitration agreement provides for the settlement of disputes by arbitration, and
(b) a dispute which involves a question of fraud arises within the provisions of such agreement, and
(c) the parties have entered into an exclusion agreement applying to any award ensuing from the reference of any such dispute,

S.3 Exclusion agreements affecting rights under S.1 and S.2 *(continued)*

then, subject to the provisions of the exclusion agreement, the High Court shall not exercise its powers under S.24(2) of the principal Act in relation to that dispute.

(4) Subject to (1) above, S.1 and S.2 shall have effect despite anything in any agreement which purports –

(a) to prohibit or restrict access to the High Court, or
(b) to restrict the jurisdiction of the High Court, or
(c) to prohibit or restrict the making of a reasoned award.

(5) An exclusion agreement is of no effect in respect of an award or a question of law arising in the course of proceedings under a statutory arbitration such as referred to in S.31(1) of the principal Act.

(6) An exclusion agreement is of no effect in respect of an award or a question of law arising in the course of proceedings under a domestic arbitration unless such agreement is entered into after the commencement of such proceedings.

(7) 'Domestic arbitration agreement' in this section means an agreement which does not provide for arbitration in a state other than the UK and to which none of the parties is based in any state other than the UK at the time such agreement is made.

S.4 Exclusion agreements not to apply in certain cases

(1) Subject to (3) below, an exclusion agreement is of no effect in respect of an award or question of law arising in the course of arbitration proceedings related to

(a) a question or claim within the jurisdiction of the Admiralty Division of the High Court, or
(b) a dispute arising from a contract of insurance, or

S.4 Exclusion agreements not to apply in certain cases *(continued)*

(c) a dispute arising from a commodity contract

unless such agreement is entered into after the commencement of such proceedings or the award or question is related to a contract governed by law other than the law of England and Wales.

(2) 'Commodity contract' in (1)(c) above means a contract

(a) for the sale of goods regularly dealt with by a commodity market or exchange in England and Wales so specified for the purpose of this section by a statutory order, and
(b) of a description so specified.

(3) By a statutory order, the provisions of (1) above

(a) shall cease to have effect, or
(b) may be modified subject to any specified conditions so as not to apply to any exclusion agreement related to an award of a description so specified

and any such order may contain such further provisions as the Secretary of State deems to be necessary or expedient.

(4) Power to make orders under (2) or (3) above shall be exercised by statutory instrument and be subject to annulment by resolution of either House of Parliament.

(5) 'Exclusion agreement' in this section means the same as in S.3.

S.5 Interlocutory Orders

(1) If a party fails to comply within the specified (or otherwise a reasonable) time with an arbitrator's or umpire's order made in the course of a reference the High Court may upon application by the arbitrator or umpire or any party make an order extending the powers of the

S.5 Interlocutory Orders
(continued)

arbitrator/umpire as provided in (2) below.

(2) Subject as may be stipulated by the High Court in such order, the arbitrator/umpire may continue with the reference on an *ex parte* basis or otherwise as would a judge of the High Court in default of appearance or other act by one of the parties.

(3) S.4(5) of the Administration of Justice Act 1970 (jurisdiction of the High Court to be exercisable by the Court of Appeal re judge-arbitrators/umpires) shall not apply to the power of the High Court to make such an order under this Section. That power shall be exercisable in references to a judge-arbitrator/umpire.

(4) Anything done by a judge-arbitrator/umpire in exercising his power under (3) above is done in his capacity as a judge of the High Court and has effect as if done by the High Court.

(5) The provisions of this Section are not affected by anything in any agreement but do not interfere with any powers given to an arbitrator/umpire in an arbitration agreement or otherwise.

(6) The terms 'judge arbitrator' and 'judge-umpire' have the same meaning as in Schedule 3 to the Administration of Justice Act 1970.

S.6 Minor amendments relating to awards and appointment of arbitrators and umpires

(1) Subsection (1) of S.8 of the principal Act is amended to provide that the required appointment of an umpire may be made at any time and shall be made forthwith upon the two arbitrators failing to agree.

(2) S.9 of the principal Act is replaced by an amended clause providing that when three arbitrators are appointed the award of any two is binding.

(3) Paragraph (c) of S.10 of the principal Act is amended by inserting 'required or are' after 'are' (line 1) and by deleting 'or where' and the rest of the paragraph.

The effect of this amendment is to reinforce the provisions whereby the appointment of an umpire or third arbitrator can be referred to the court in default of such appointment being made by the parties or the two arbitrators concerned.

(4) New subsection (2) is added to S.10 of the principal Act to provide that in the event of unwillingness or failure by a third party nominated in an arbitration agreement to appoint an arbitrator within the time stipulated or otherwise, a party may serve a notice on such third party requiring him to make such appointment and if it is not then made within seven clear days the High Court or a judge thereof may upon application appoint an arbitrator to act as though he had been appointed in accordance with the agreement.

S.7 Application and interpretation of certain provisions of Part I of principal Act

(1) Part I of the principal Act shall have effect as if the following provisions of that Act had been amended to incorporate the foregoing provisions of this Act:
S.14: Interim awards.
S.28: Terms as to costs of orders.
S.30: Crown to be bound.
S.31: Application to statutory arbitrations.
S.32: Meaning of 'arbitration agreement'.

(2) Subsections (2) and (3) of S.29 of the principal Act apply to the determination of when an arbitration is commenced in relation to this Act.

(3) The reference to statutory arbitrations in subsection (1) of S.31 of the principal Act does not apply to arbitrations under S.92 of the County Courts Act 1959.

Accordingly, nothing in Part I of the principal Act applies to such arbitrations.

S.8 Short title, commencement, repeals and extent

(1) The title of this Act is the Arbitration Act 1979.

(2) This Act shall come into operation as a whole (or in part) on such day (or days) as may be ordered by the Secretary of State; such order may also contain such further provisions as appear to the Secretary of State to be necessary or expedient. *(See Note (D) above.)*

(3) In consequence of the foregoing provisions, the following provisions are repealed

(a) in paragraph (c) of S.10 of the principal Act, the words 'or where' to the end of the paragraph,
(b) the whole of S.21 of the principal Act,

(c) in paragraph 9 of the Schedule 3 to the Administration of Justice Act 1970, the words '21(1) and (2)' in sub-paragraph (1) and the whole of subparagraph (2).

(4) This Act applies only to England and Wales.

PART III
TYPICAL DOCUMENTATION

(1) *Ad Hoc* Arbitration Agreement

(adaptable for general use)

See Notes for Guidance below

In the matter of the Arbitration Acts 1950 to 1979 (A)
and
in the matter of an arbitration
between *(Name)*
of *(Address)* – Claimant (B)
and *(Name)*
of *(Address)* – Respondent (C)

MEMORANDUM OF AGREEMENT made this day of 19 (D)
between (E)
of
(hereinafter referred to as 'the Claimant') of the one part
and (F)
of
(hereinafter referred to as 'the Respondent') of the other part

WHEREAS a dispute or difference has arisen and still subsists between the parties hereto (G)

It is hereby agreed by and between the said parties that –

subject as hereinafter provided all questions differences or disputes arising out of or in connection with the Agreement/Contract between them dated (hereinafter referred to as 'the Trading Agreement/Contract') shall be and are hereby referred (H/1)

subject as hereinafter provided the matter/s set out in the First Schedule herein arising out of or in connection with the Agreement/Contract between them dated (hereinafter referred to as 'the Trading Agreement/Contract') shall be and is/are hereby referred (H/2) subject to the rights and obligations of the parties made therein the matter/s in dispute in the action now pending in the Queen's Bench Division of Her Majesty's High Court of Justice *(name)* District Registry between the said parties and bearing Reference Number *(number)* be and is/are hereby referred (H/3)

to the arbitration and final decision of (I)

Mr/Mrs/Miss *(Names in full)* (J)
of *(Address)*
who shall upon acceptance of such appointment be the arbitrator hereunder or in the event of his/her death or inability or unwillingness so to act to

a person nominated for that purpose by the President or a Vice-President for the time being of *(name of body)* (hereinafter referred to as 'the nominating Body') upon written application by either or both parties and upon acceptance of appointment accordingly such person shall be the arbitrator hereunder (K)

a judge-arbitrator under S.4 of the Administration of Justice Act 1970 (L)

in place of the person so designated previously herein (M)

ALWAYS PROVIDED that:

1 neither Party shall invoke the provisions of this Agreement until fourteen days after he has given written notice to the other Party of his intention to do so and specifying the matter/s said to be in dispute (N)
2 the provision/s of Section/s No/s *(state numbers)* of the Arbitration Act 1950 and of Section/s No/s *(state numbers)* of the Arbitration Act 1979 shall not apply to any proceedings arising from this Agreement (P)
3 the provision/s set out in the Second Schedule hereto shall apply to any proceedings arising from this Agreement (Q)
4 any such proceedings shall be otherwise conducted in accordance with and subject to the Rules of *(name of body)* (hereinafter referred to as 'the administering Authority') last published at the date on which the arbitrator is appointed under this Agreement (R)
5 the Party who applies to the nominating Body as aforesaid shall pay any fee prescribed by that Body in respect of the (S)

registration of such application and/or any related nomination

6 the Parties jointly and severally will be responsible for –

(a) paying the reasonable fees and expenses of the arbitrator and/or administering Authority in accordance with the said Rules and taking up any Award within fourteen days of receipt of notice of its publication and (T)

(b) providing adequate security for the due payment of such fees and expenses if the arbitrator so requires (U)

THE FIRST SCHEDULE REFERRED TO: MATTER/S IN DISPUTE

The arbitrator shall determine what sum/s if any is/are due from either party to the other in respect of – (V)

(1)

(2)

(3)

– under the said Trading Agreement/Contract

THE SECOND SCHEDULE REFERRED TO: SUPPLEMENTARY PROVISION/S (W)

1 Any Award published in respect of any proceedings arising on this Agreement shall include the substance of the reasons for the arbitrator's findings as therein expressed

2 A shorthand note (or tape-recording) shall be made of the proceedings at any hearing subject to such note (or recording) being transcribed wholly or in part only as may be ordered by the arbitrator

3 The arbitrator shall adjudge the matter/s in dispute and publish his award solely on the basis of documentary evidence and written submissions by the parties made by such date as ordered by the arbitrator

IN WITNESS WHEREOF the said parties have hereunto set their hands the day and year first above written

Signed by
or on behalf of
CLAIMANT (X)

WITNESSED BY –

(Signature) (X)

(Address)

(Designation)

Signed by
or on behalf of
RESPONDENT (X)

WITNESSED BY –
(Signature) (X)
(Address)

(Designation)

Notes

(A) This heading incorporates the 1975 Act; if it is not applicable, insert '1950 and 1979' in place of '1950 to 1979'. If Scottish law applies, insert 'Arbitration (Scotland) Act 1894' in lieu of '1950 to 1979' and adapt otherwise as necessary.
(B) Name (only) of Claimant.
(C) Name (only) of Respondent.
(D) Insert date after both parties have signed the Agreement.
(E) Name and address of Claimant.
(F) Name and address of Respondent.
(G) Omit this statement if Agreement is made before dispute arises.
(H) Typical alternative clauses are indicated as (H/1)–(H/2)–(H/3); (H/1) is appropriate in pre-dispute agreements; (H/2) may be used when (G) is incorporated in post-dispute agreements; (H/3) is applicable only when related proceedings have been initiated in the court and the Judge has ordered that the matters in dispute, or any of them, be referred to an arbitrator.
(I) This provision must be included in all cases.
(J) If the parties wish to pre-agree the arbitrator, his/her name can be identified as indicated; (J) should always be followed by (K) and (M).
(K) This provision can stand alone – omitting (J)–(L)–(M) – and is the best arrangement for most pre-dispute agreements.
(L) This provision is an up-dating of the option under S.11 of the 1950 Act; it can be used alone or in association with (J) and (M).
(M) Include when (J) is used with (K) or (L).
(N) Neither party should act without giving the other due notice.
(P) Such exclusions are optional – subject as provided in the relevant Acts. Exclusions under S.3 of the 1979 Act can be made only *after* a dispute has arisen and proceedings have been commenced.
(Q) Such supplementary provisions are optional – subject as aforesaid.
(R) The Rules to be adopted could be either of the following, or any others agreed by the parties: Rules of the London Court of International Arbitration, the UNCITRAL Rules, the rules of a particular Trade Association or institutional arbitration scheme.
(S)
(T) These provisions are self-explanatory.
(U)
(V) This provision is applicable only to post-dispute agreements when (G) and (H/2) are also incorporated.
(W) Omit *'SECOND'* when no *FIRST SCHEDULE* appears; the same applies to (Q) above. The examples given are typical only; (2) and (3) are mutually exclusive.
(X) The attestation provisions are self-explanatory.

(2) *Ad hoc* Arbitration Agreement: Short Form

(applicable to post-dispute agreement in which the arbitrator can be named)

See Notes to (1), p. 122, and apply as appropriate

In the matter of the Arbitration Acts 1950 to 1979
and
in the matter of an arbitration
between *(Name)*
of *(Address)* – Claimant
and *(Name)*
of *(Address)* – Respondent

MEMORANDUM OF AGREEMENT
made this day of 19
between *(Name)*
(the above named Claimant) of the one part
and *(Name)*
(the above named Respondent) of the other part

WHEREAS a dispute or difference has arisen and still subsists between the parties hereto arising on an Agreement between them dated ('the trading Agreement') whereby the above named Claimant/Respondent ('the Seller'/'the Contractor') undertook to *(describe undertaking/s)* and the above named Respondent/Claimant ('the Buyer'/'the Employer') undertook to pay for such goods/services/works

It is hereby agreed by and between the said parties that

subject as hereinafter provided all disputes and matters in difference whatsoever arising out of or in connection with the said trading Agreement be and are hereby referred to the award order and final determination *(Name)* of *(Address)* (hereinafter referred to as 'the arbitrator') or in the event of his/her death or unwillingness or inability so to act of a person agreed by the parties hereto to be the arbitrator in place of the said *(Name)*

ALWAYS PROVIDED that if no such further agreement has been achieved within *(number)* days of a written Notice by one party to the other requesting such agreement either party may apply to the Chartered Institute of Arbitrators for a nomination by the President or a Vice-President for the time being of that Body of a person to be the arbitrator in place of the said *(name)* and upon acceptance of appointment accordingly such person shall be the arbitrator hereunder

And it is further agreed by and between the said parties that –

1 any proceedings arising on this Agreement shall be governed by the Rules/Regulations for the Conduct of Arbitrations last published by *(Body)* at the date of this Agreement

2 the parties or either of them will

   (a) pay the reasonable fees and expenses of the arbitrator whether the proceedings reach a Hearing or not

   (b) provide adequate security for such payment if the Arbitrator so requires

   (c) take up any award within fourteen days of receipt of notice of its publication

3 *(Here insert an 'exclusion agreement', if so agreed – but only in post-dispute agreements)*

IN WITNESS WHEREOF the said parties have hereunto set their hands the day and year first above written

Signed by or
on behalf of
CLAIMANT ....

WITNESSED BY –
(Signature) ....
(Address)

(Designation)

Signed by or
on behalf of
RESPONDENT ....

WITNESSED BY –
(Signature) ....
(Address)

(Designation)

Arbitrator's acceptance of appointment

I, *(name)* , *the arbitrator identified / as provided /* *
in the above agreement dated 19
between – Claimant
and – Respondent
hereby agree to hear and determine the matter/s in dispute referred to me in accordance with the said agreement

(Signed)
(Arbitrator)
Date:

*Omit 'as provided' when acceptance is by the person named in the Agreement.

Notes

See Notes to (1) and apply as appropriate.

(3) Arbitration Agreement in Conditions of Contract

See Notes for Guidance below

If any question, difference or dispute shall at any time arise between the parties in respect of the validity or construction of this Agreement or as to rights liabilities or duties of the parties under this Agreement and the same is not resolved within fourteen days of written notice thereof having been given by one party to the other such question difference or dispute shall be and is hereby referred to the arbitration and final decision of

(Named person) of *(address)* (A/1)
or in the event of his/her death or inability or unwillingness so to act of

a person to be agreed between the parties within *(number)* (A/2)
days of the said written notice having been given or in the event of such agreement not having been achieved of

a person to be nominated on the written application of either party (B)
by the President or a Vice-President for the time being of
(Body)
ALWAYS PROVIDED that the arbitration proceedings shall be conducted in accordance with and subject to the Rules of *(Body)* current at the date of this Contract/Agreement. (D)

Notes

(A) A/1 and A/2 are alternative options; A/1 may be useful for short-term transactions but A/2 is recommended for general use.
(B) This should follow A/1 or A/2 in all cases.
(C) Any appropriate Body may be named.
(D) The chosen Rules need not be those of the nominating Body, e.g. The nominating Body could be the Royal College of Veterinary Surgeons while the Rules, if any, could be those of the Chartered Institute of Arbitrators, the London Court of International Arbitration, UNCITRAL, or a particular Trade Association.

(4) First Order of Directions

See Notes for Guidance below

In the matter of the Arbitration Acts 1950 to 1979 (A)
and
in the matter of an arbitration
between (*Name*) – Claimant (B)
and (*Name*) – Respondent (C)

ORDER OF DIRECTIONS No 1
issued the *day of* 19 (D)

By consent (E/1)

Upon hearing the parties (E/2)

Upon hearing the solicitors/advocates/for the parties – (E/3)
the Claimant being represented by (*Name*) and the Respondent by (*Name*)

The following directions are hereby given and it is ordered: (F)

1 That all communications in the above matter between either Party and the Arbitrator be confirmed in writing and copied to the other Party. (G)
2 That Pleadings be served as follows – (H)
   (a) Points of Claim: by Claimant within (*number*) days of the date hereof
   (b) Points of Defence to Claim and Points of Counter-claim, if any: by Respondent within (*number*) days of service of Points of Claim
   (c) Points of Reply to Defence to Claim and Points of Defence to Counter-claim, if any: by Claimant within (*number*) days of service of Points of Defence to Claim
   (d) Points of Reply to Defence to Counter-claim: by

Respondent within *(number)* days of service of Points of Defence to Counter-claim, if any.

3 That the Claimant and Respondent do each within *(number)* days of completing the service of Pleadings deliver to the other a list of the relevant documents which are or have been in their respective possession, custody or power and that inspection be afforded by each to the other within *(number)* days thereafter. (I)

4 That copies of the Pleadings and related documents correspondence and other papers be delivered to me / by each Party as and when he serves the same upon the other Party. / by the Claimant in one or more numbered and indexed bundles not less than seven days before the first day of the Hearing. (J)

5 That all relevant figures be agreed (as figures only) to the fullest extent possible before the Hearing. (K)

6 That the Hearing be commenced on / such date and at such place and time as I shall further direct. / *(date)* at such place and time as I shall further direct. / *(date)* at *(place of Hearing)*. (L)

7 That *(name)* arrange that suitable accommodation is available for the Hearing and inform me and *(name)* the location thereof not less than *(number)* days before the first day of the Hearing. (M)

8 That *(name)* arrange that a record of the proceedings at the Hearing be made by a / short-hand writer / tape-recorder / and for transcribing such record or any part thereof as I may require and order for my sole use. (N)

9 That expert witnesses be limited to *(number)* on each side. (P)

10 That the costs of applying for and complying with this Order be costs in the arbitration. (Q)

11 That either Party has liberty to apply. (R)

Given under my hand the day/year first above written

....

(Arbitrator in the above matter)

TO: *(Name/address)*

– Claimant/Solicitor/s for Claimant

AND: *(Name/address)*

– Respondent/Solicitor/s for Respondent

Notes

(A) This heading incorporates the 1975 Act; see Note (A) in (1) (p. 122).
(B) Name of Claimant.
(C) Name of Respondent.
(D) Insert date of issue.
(E) Use E/1 if all matters ordered have been mutually agreed with and between the parties. Use E/2 in respect of any orders made at the discretion of the arbitrator after hearing the parties.
Use E/3 in similar circumstances to E/2 but when parties have been represented.
(F) This is a standard lead-in.
(G) It is essential that all parties and the arbitrator are kept fully informed about every communication in the proceedings between the parties (except, of course, those 'without prejudice') and between either of them and the arbitrator.
(H) If Pleadings are to be exchanged as part of the proceedings, the fact and the date-table must be 'ordered'.
(I) The list compiled by each party should include a reference to every item of relevance – whether relied upon by the party in preparing his case or not – and whether or not he claims that it is 'privileged'.
(J) Some arbitrators like to receive copies of the Pleadings as each is served – thereby knowing that the date-table is (or is not) being complied with; others prefer not to have any such details until just before the Hearing commences, relying on the parties (or either of them) to apply for a 'chasing-up' order if necessary.
(K) To save time at the Hearing, any figures which can be agreed (as figures – without admission/denial of liability) should be agreed between the parties and reported, as such, in the Pleadings or at the Hearing.
(L) It is not usual to prescribe the date/time/place of the Hearing in Order No. 1, but the option to do so exists.
(M) Accommodation for the Hearing may be arranged by the arbitrator or, in certain circumstances, by the administering authority; in some cases it may be convenient for (say) the Claimant to make the arrangements – which the arbitrator can confirm by a further order if necessary.
(N) The question whether and, if so, by what means a record of the proceedings at the Hearing shall be made is another potential subject to be included in Order No 1; the arbitrator is only concerned with the transcription of such parts as he requires for his own use although, of course, the parties or either of them, can have as much transcription made as they consider necessary.
(P) The arbitrator should ensure that each party is aware of the other's intentions about the presentation of his case, both as regards advocacy and the calling of expert evidence.
(Q) This is standard and makes clear the entitlement of the parties to include the associated costs in their respective bills.
(R) This is standard and allows either party to apply for an order to vary the terms of the above order for the reasons to be given; normally, provided any such application is reasonable, it should be granted – particularly when not objected to by the other party.

(5) Expert's Report/ Proof of Evidence

In the matter of the Arbitration Acts 1950 and 1979
and
in the matter of an arbitration
between *(Name)* – Claimant
and *(Name)* – Respondent

REPORT by *(Name/Degrees/Qualifications)*

1 *QUALIFICATIONS/EXPERIENCE*
(Here include a factual statement about the person making the Report, without over-stating (or under-rating) his/her virtues and competence)
2 *MATERIAL QUESTIONS*
(Here list the material questions referred to the Expert and/or emerging from his perusal of correspondence and other papers)
3 *DOCUMENTS EXAMINED*
(Here list the documents supplied and/or others seen in the course of investigating the matter/s referred for the Expert's examination and opinion)
4 *CLAIMANT'S (OR RESPONDENT'S) RIGHTS UNDER THE CONTRACT*
(Here summarise the (relevant) rights and expectations of the Claimant under the contract between him and the Respondent – or vice versa – cross-referenced to specific clauses of the related conditions of contract and related documents)
5 *CLAIMANT'S (OR RESPONDENT'S) GRIEVANCE/S*
(Here outline the Claimant's (or Respondent's) grievance/s and relate them to his rights and expectations as outlined under 4 above)
6 *COMMENTS ON BUNDLE OF AGREED DOCUMENTS*
(Here enter the comments, if any, which are necessary/appropriate)

7 *COMMENTS ON DOCUMENTS NOT AGREED*
(Here enter the comments, if any, which are appropriate)

8 *COMMENTS ON (Define particular document/s)*
(Here enter the comments which may be necessary/appropriate with reference to particular document/s e.g. Tender Document/s, Specification, Bills of Quantities)

9 *COMMENTS ON POINTS OF CLAIM*
(Here enter comments as may be necessary/appropriate)

10 *COMMENTS ON POINTS OF DEFENCE AND OTHER PLEADINGS*
(Here follow with similar Sections in respect of each stage of the Pleadings)

11 *INSPECTION/TESTING OF (Materials/Goods/Workmanship/Land/Property)*
(Here state date/s and other details of inspection/testing by or under the directions of the writer, with observed or measured result/s)

12 *CONCLUSIONS/RECOMMENDATIONS*
(Here summarise the conclusions reached and any ensuing recommendations offered by the writer)

and I so advise

(Signature)

(town/city of issue)

(Date)

Notes

(a) The format and content of any such Report/Proof of Evidence is entirely within the discretion of the author; however, this document can be used as a 'check-list' of the matters which could be relevant.
(b) Except for No. 1, the sub-headings shown above are only typical; some, obviously, are mutually exclusive and other sub-headings may be necessary in particular circumstances.
(c) In addition to presenting the details in a clear, concise and easy-to-refer-to form, a journalistic style of presentation in plain English should be the aim, avoiding clichés and other jargon, but not shrinking from the use of technical terms in so far as this is necessary and unavoidable.
(d) It should always be kept in mind that the resultant document is likely to be made available to 'the other side' as well as to the arbitrator (or judge) at the hearing (or trial). Therefore, everything stated must be capable of being 'proved' and defended, if necessary, under cross-examination.

(6) Points of Claim

In the matter of the Arbitration Acts 1950 and 1979
and
in the matter of an arbitration
between *(Name)* – Claimant
and *(Name)* – Respondent

POINTS OF CLAIM

1 *Preamble*

1.1 The matter/s in dispute arise/s in connection with an Agreement between the parties dated which incorporates the conditions of the JCT Standard Form of Building Contract, *WITH QUANTITIES* (1963 Edition; 1977 Revision) which provide, inter alia, for the settlement by arbitration of any dispute which cannot be resolved by agreement between the parties.

1.2 By the said Agreement the Claimant ('the Contractor' therein) undertook to execute the Works therein defined and the Respondent ('the Employer' therein) undertook to pay for such work as provided therein.

1.3 The heads of claim are:

(a) Further extension of time,
(b) Additional payment in respect of loss and expense due to delay,
(c) Money due but not paid and interest thereon,
(d) Costs in the arbitration.

1.4 These matters are further detailed herein.

2 *Further extension of time*

2.1 Claimant holds and has always maintained that the total delay in completing the Works was due to factors for which an extension of time should be granted under Clause 23 of the conditions of contract.

2.2 Accordingly, Claimant requests that the date for completion be extended to coincide with the certified date of practical completion.

2.3 The grounds for this request are detailed in the correspondence; in particular, the Memorandum dated *(date)* and the letters the Claimant wrote to the Architect on *(date)* and *(date)* respectively.

2.4 The general position is illustrated by the Chart attached hereto.

3 *Additional payment in respect of loss/expense*

3.1 Delays occurred as follows

(a)	Delivery of facing bricks	9 weeks
(b)	Delivery of sanitary appliances	13 weeks
(c)	Additional decoration work	2 weeks
(d)	*Total delay*	24 weeks

3.2 A fair and reasonable assessment of the extra costs incurred by the Claimant as a consequence of such delay is attached hereto.

3.3 Accordingly, the amount requested is: £ *(sum)*.

4 *Money due but not paid*

4.1 Certificates and payments issued to date are as follows:

(a) CERTIFICATES			(b) PAYMENTS REC'D		
No.	*Date*	*Amount (£)*	*No.*	*Date*	*Amount (£)*
1	11 Aug	*(sum)*	1	18 Aug	*(sum)*
2	5 Oct	*(sum)*	2	20 Oct	*(sum)*
3	21 Dec	*(sum)*			
4	19 Feb	*(sum)*	3	10 Apr	*(sum)*
5	9 Jul	*(sum)*			
		£ *(sum)*			£ *(sum)*

4.2 Outstanding balance due to Claimant:

Amount of Claimant's final account	£ *(sum)*
Less: Amount paid to date (see 4.1(b) above)	£ *(sum)*
Balance due	£ *(sum)*

4.3 The said balance is made up as follows:

(a) Retention	£ *(sum)*
(b) Under-certified	£ *(sum)*
(c) Certified but not paid	£ *(sum)*
Total	£ *(sum)*

4.4 Accordingly, Claimant requests payment of the amount due but not yet paid – that is to say, the sum of £ *(sum)* mentioned in 4.2 above.

4.5 In addition, Claimant requests payment in respect of interest related to such amount, calculated at commercial rates, as follows:

(a) On £ *(sum)* (amount of Certificate No. 3) for, say, 90 days
(b) On £ *(sum)* (amount of Certificate No. 4) for, say, 30 days
(c) On £ *(sum)* (amount of Certificate No. 5) for, say, the period from 14 days after 9 July
(d) On £ *(sum)* (the balance) for, say, the period from the expiry of the defects liability period on 9 August.

5 *Costs*

5.1 Claimant requests payment in respect of the additional costs he has incurred (including professional advice and services) in connection with the pursuance of his request for settlement of the matters in dispute.

5.2 He also requests to be indemnified in respect of the costs of the arbitration.

6 *Appendices hereto*

6.1 Chart showing relevant events and other details.

6.2 Statement of Claimant's loss and expense.

Served this day of 19
by

(Agent for Claimant)

Notes

(a) The Appendices referred to in Para. 6 above are not included herein.
(b) This example is not related to any of those in other sections of Part III and is not offered as the only or best format in all circumstances.

(7) Scott Schedule

In the matter of the arbitration
between *(Name)* – Claimant
and *(Name)* – Respondent

SCOTT SCHEDULE initiated by Claimant in accordance with Arbitrator's Order No.					Dated	SHEET No.
ITEM	CLAIMANT'S CLAIM		RESPONDENT'S REJOINDER		CLAIMANT'S REPLY	ARBITRATOR'S NOTES
	DETAILS	AMOUNT (£)	DETAILS	AMOUNT (£)		
(a)	(b)	(c)	(d)	(e)	(f)	(g)

See Notes overleaf

Notes

(A) The typical format shown is intended to illustrate the essential features of a Scott Schedule. It is not mandatory and any appropriate presentation can be adopted to suit the circumstances of a particular case. For example, more and/or wider columns could be provided by using A3 paper.

(B) In some circumstances, a Scott Schedule could be the medium by which the details of a claim (or counter-claim) are brought into the Pleadings but this could become too detailed and, therefore, congested. It is usually more convenient to set out the contentions in the Points of Claim (or Points of Counter-claim) and Points of Defence, and, consequently, to regard the Scott Schedule as a summary (only) of the essential details.

(C) In most cases, a Scott Schedule is initiated by the Claimant but, if there is a counter-claim, the Respondent can take the initiative – unless either or both of the parties are ordered to do so by the arbitrator. In any event, the 'initiator' drafts the schedule and enters the necessary details in columns (a), (b) and (c). It then goes to the other party whose denial and/or counter-proposals are entered in columns (d) and (e) before it goes back to the initiator – who may then, if he wishes, make use of column (f) for recording any comments on what is entered in columns (d) and (e).

(D) The arbitrator should be kept informed of the processing of the Scott Schedule in accordance with any requirements he may have specified with regard to the interlocutory proceedings.

(E) In disputes arising on contracts for building work, a Scott Schedule is often used to bring together the respective allegations of the parties with reference to such matters as: the ordering of extra work, payment for extra work, the omission of work and the value thereof, rectification of defects and the cost thereof if executed by a third party, over-charging for work executed, the computation of fluctuations in the basic cost of labour, materials and insurances, and the extra cost of delays and/or disruption in executing the work.

(F) A Scott Schedule is sometimes referred to as an 'Official Referee's Schedule'.

(8) Request for Further and Better Particulars of Points of Claim

In the matter of the Arbitration Acts 1950 and 1979
and
in the matter of an arbitration
between *(Name)* – Claimant
and *(Name)* – Respondent

REQUEST FOR FURTHER AND BETTER PARTICULARS OF POINTS OF CLAIM AND RELATED SCOTT SCHEDULE

1 *Under paragraph 2*
of the implicit allegation that the Respondent is in breach of the Sub-Contract:

(1) Identify all terms of the Sub-Contract alleged to have been broken.
(2) Particularise every breach of contract relied on.

2 *Under claim no. 2: dayworks*
Of each hourly rate claimed in respect of dayworks, state how this is calculated or made up, and further particularise the alleged entitlement to this rate by reference to the Sub-Contract terms.

3 *Under claim no. 3(c): delay and extension of time*
Please give full particulars of every instruction and/or variation to the Sub-Contract Works relied on in support of this claim, identifying by date and reference number (if appropriate) the instruction and/or the Variation Order.

4 *(continue as necessary)*

8 *Under claim no. 10*
Please quantify the damages claimed hereunder with full details thereof.

Served this day of 19
by

(Solicitor/s for the Respondent)

Note

This example is not related to any of those in other sections of Part III and is not offered as the only or best format appropriate in all circumstances.

(9) Points of Defence and Counter-Claim

In the matter of the Arbitration Acts 1950 and 1979
and
in the matter of an arbitration

between	*(Name)*	– Claimant
and	*(Name)*	– Respondent

POINTS OF DEFENCE AND COUNTER-CLAIM

Points of defence

1 The basic obligations of the Respondent as Sub-Contractor referred to within Sub-Sections ( ) to ( ) of the Points of Claim are admitted but, in doing so, the Respondent states:

(a)
(b)

2 The alleged obligations referred to within sub-sections ( ) to ( ) of the Points of Claim are not accepted or admitted; they are not incorporated in the terms and conditions of the Agreement between the parties or subsequently agreed between them.

3 The Respondent denies that he is in breach of contract as alleged in Section 4 of the Points of Claim or at all and, in particular, denies the statements and claims in Section ( ) of the Points of Claim.

4 *(continue as necessary)*

9 If, contrary to his contention, the Respondent is held to be liable to the Claimant for the sum claimed or any other sum or sums, he (the Respondent) will seek to set off against the same such sums as are held to be due to him in respect of his Counter-claim hereinafter pleaded.

Points of counter-claim:

1 The Respondent repeats paragraphs (/) of the Points of Defence.

2 The Claimant is in breach of contract in so far as he –

(a) failed to pay the Respondent in accordance with the contract conditions;
(b) failed to provide materials for the Sub-Contract Works of suitable quality and/or at the proper times and in the required quantities to permit the Respondent to maintain the regular progress of the Sub-Contract Works;
(c) failed to provide and/or maintain on the site of the Works the plant which was necessary to maintain the regular progress of the Sub-Contract Works.

3 By reason of the said breaches of contract by the Claimant –

(a) the regular progress of the Sub-Contract Works was materially hindered by the acts, omissions and defaults of the Claimant (as the Contractor), his servants or agents and other sub-contractors employed in connection with the execution of the Works;
(b) the Respondent was prevented from completing the Sub-Contract Works;
(c) the Respondent has suffered loss and incurred expense amounting to £ *(sum)* – full particulars of which are set out in the Appendix hereto – and claims Damages accordingly.

WHEREFORE the Respondent counter-claims –

1 Damages for breach of contract in the sum of £ *(sum as above)* (*(amount in words)*),

2 Interest thereon at commercial rates.

Served this day of 19
by

(Agent for the Respondent)

Notes

(a) The Appendix mentioned in 3(c) above is not included in this example.
(b) This example is not related to any of those in other Sections of Part III and is not offered as the only or best format appropriate in all circumstances.

(10) Points of Reply and Defence to Counter-Claim

In the matter of the Arbitration Acts 1950 and 1979
and
in the matter of an arbitration
between *(Name)* – Claimant
and *(Name)* – Respondent

POINTS OF REPLY AND DEFENCE TO COUNTER-CLAIM

Points of reply:

1 Save in so far as the Points of Defence consist of admissions the Claimant joins issue with the Respondent in respect of the allegations contained therein.

2 In particular, the Claimant takes issue with the Respondent with regard to the allegations made in paragraph/s (/) concerning work executed on a daywork basis and, in that connection, makes the following further observations:

(a)
(b)
(c)

3 Furthermore, the Claimant takes issue with the Respondent over his allegations with regard to:

1 Scott Schedule Item/s No/s (/)
(Say why)
2 Responsibility for the preparation of a final account for the Sub-Contract Works
(Say why)
3 The payment and/or withholding of monies due to the Claimant
(Say why)

4 The allegation that the Claimant is responsible for the loss of or damage to materials which it was the responsibility of the Respondent to provide.
(Say why)

Points of defence to counter-claim:

1 Save as expressly admitted herein, the Claimant denies such and every allegation made in the Counter-claim as if set out herein and denied seriatim.

2 The Claimant rejects the cost factors mentioned in paragraph (No.) of the Points of Defence, both as to details and implications; the reasonable costs (including disbursements and expenses) related to week-end working are included in the contra-charges previously agreed by the parties.

3 The Claimant accepts partial responsibility for the damage referred to in paragraph (No.) of the Points of Counter-claim and, therefore, admits liability for a proportion of the reasonable cost of rectification; he denies that the total cost stated by the Respondent is a reasonable one or that his (the Claimant's) liability is for the amount alleged by the Respondent.

Served this day of 19
by

(Agent for the Claimant)

Note

This example is not related to any of those in other Sections of Part III and is not offered as the only or best format appropriate in all circumstances.

(11) List of Documents

In the matter of the Arbitration Acts 1950 and 1979
and
in the matter of an arbitration
between *(Name)* – Claimant
and *(Name)* – Respondent

RESPONDENT'S LIST OF DOCUMENTS

1 This is a list of the documents which are or have been in the possession, custody or power of the Respondent relating to the matters in question in this Arbitration; it is served in accordance with Order No. *(number)* issued by the Arbitrator herein on *(date)*.
2 The Respondent has in his possession, custody or power the documents mentioned in Schedule I hereto.
3 The Respondent objects to the production of any of the documents referred to in Part 2 of the said Schedule I on the grounds that by their nature they are privileged.
4 The Respondent has had but does not now have in his possession, custody or power the documents referred to in Schedule II hereto; those documents were last in his custody, possession or power on or about the dates they bear.
5 Neither the Respondent nor his solicitor/s nor any other person on his behalf has now or ever had in his/their custody, possession or power any document of any description whatsoever related to any matter in question in this Arbitration other than the documents mentioned in Schedules I and II hereto.

SCHEDULE I: PART 1		
ITEM No.	DESCRIPTION	DATE
	(Here list each and every relevant item)	

SCHEDULE I: PART 2

ITEM No.	DESCRIPTION	DATE
1	Correspondence between the Respondent and his solicitor/s arising in contemplation and/or pursuance of this Arbitration.	Various
2	Correspondence and other documents prepared for the purpose of obtaining and supplying to the Respondent's solicitor/s the necessary information and evidence to enable him (them) to advise the Respondent and to conduct the Respondent's Defence and Counter-claim.	Various
3	Respondent's solicitor's attendance notes, memoranda and other such documentation	Various

SCHEDULE II

ITEM No.	DESCRIPTION	DATE
–	The originals of the documents described in Schedule I Part 1 as copies of correspondence and other documents.	

Take notice that the documents listed above (except those in Schedule I Part 2) may be inspected at *(address)* on reasonable notice and between the hours of 9.30 am and 4.00 pm on any normal working day.

Served this day of 19
by

Solicitor/s for the Respondent

(12) Endorsement of 'Sealed Offer' Envelope

See Notes for Guidance below

In the matter of the arbitration (A)
between *(Name)* – Claimant
and *(Name)* – Respondent

This envelope contains a copy of the letter dated sent by the Respondent to the Claimant (or by the Claimant to the Respondent) (B)

It should be opened when the arbitrator has decided the matter/s in issue and before he decides the respective liabilities of the parties for the related costs (B/1)

*This envelope contains a document supplied by the Respondent (*or *Claimant) to comply with the arbitrator's order No. (number) dated* (C)

Notes

(a) An appropriate endorsement would be: (A) + (B) *or* (A) + (C).
(b) Alternative (B) is applicable to cases in which the initiative is taken by the Respondent – or the Claimant in respect of a counter-claim; the insertion of (B/1) should not be necessary but may be prudent in certain circumstances.
(c) Alternative (C) is applicable to cases in which the arbitrator has directed that an envelope be handed to him containing *either* a copy of any offer to settle *or* a declaration that no such offer has been made.
(d) In 'administered arbitrations' the sealed envelope should be handed to the Registrar or other appropriate official of the administering authority; in other cases it should be handed to the arbitrator.

(13) Award (General)

See Notes for Guidance below

In the matter of the Arbitration Acts 1950 to 1979 (A)
and
in the matter of an arbitration
under the rules of *(Body)* (B)
between – (C)
of
– Claimant
and – (D)
of
– Respondent

THIS IS THE FINAL AWARD of me (Full Names of Arbitrator) *of* (Address) *the Arbitrator appointed to hear and determine the above matter made and published in* (Town/City) *the* *day of* 19

1 *WHEREAS* – On the day of 19 an Agreement ('the Trading Agreement' / 'the Building Contract') was entered into between the above named parties whereby the Claimant ('the Seller' / 'the Contractor') undertook to *(State obligations)* and the Respondent ('the Buyer' / 'the Employer') undertook to *(State obligations)* (E) (F) (G)

2 *AND* – the said / Trading Agreement / Building Contract / provides (inter alia) that – (H)
(1) any dispute or difference whatsoever arising under or in relation to that / Agreement / Contract / including its validity construction and performance shall be determined by a sole arbitrator and
(2) if either party fails to concur in the appointment of such arbitrator within fourteen days of receiving a written request from the other party to do so such appointment shall be made by the President or a Vice-President for the time being of *(Body)* upon receiving a written request from either party to do so and (I)

(3) any proceedings ensuing therefrom shall be conducted under and in accordance with the Rules of *(Body)* last issued at the date of the said / Agreement / Contract / application. (J)

3 *AND*
WHEREAS – a dispute having arisen and the parties having been unable to concur in the appointment of an arbitrator the Claimant applied accordingly for the nomination of an arbitrator on *(Date)*

4 *AND* – the President of *(Body)* nominated me *(Full names)* on *(Date)* for appointment as sole arbitrator to hear and determine the matters in dispute and I duly accepted that appointment and took jurisdiction on *(Date)* (I)

5 *AND* – I was requested by the / Claimant / Respondent / parties to include the reason/s for my decision/s in my award as provided in S.1(6)(a) of the Arbitration Act 1979 (K)

6 *AND* – the parties entered into an Exclusion Agreement on *(date)* under the provisions of S.3(1) of the Arbitration Act 1979. (K)

7 *AND* – the parties / appeared / were represented by their respective advocates (*(Name)* appearing for the Claimant and *(Name)* appearing for the Respondent) / and made their submissions before me at the Hearing in *(Town/City)* on *(Date/s)* (L)

8 *AND* – having read the documents and heard the evidence and oral submissions put to me / by / on behalf of / the parties at the said Hearing I / inspected the *(Define)* being the subject of the dispute in the presence of *(Names)* on *(Date)* and / thereupon closed the Hearing. (M)

9 *AND*
WHEREAS – the Claimant claims: (N)

(a) the sum of £________ in respect of *(details)*
(b) the sum of £________ in respect of *(details)*
(c) the sum of £________ in respect of *(details)*
– and denies liability in respect of the Respondent's counter-claim

10 *AND* – the Respondent counter-claims: (O)
(a) the sum of £________ in respect of *(details)*
– and denies liability for the said claims

11 *AND* – each party also claims for interest and his costs in the reference and asks to be indemnified by the other in respect of the costs of the arbitration proceedings

12 *Now I (Names) the Arbitrator appointed as aforesaid do hereby adjudge and award as follows –*

1 *I FIND AND HOLD THAT –*

(a) the Claimant fails in his claim for *(details as 7(a) above)* / for the reason that *(give reason/s)* and this is Dismissed (P)

(b) the Claimant's claim for *(details as 7(b) above)* succeeds in the sum of £________/ for the reason that *(give reason/s)*

(c) the Claimant's claim for ....

(d) the Respondent's counter-claim for *(details as 8(a) above)* succeeds in the sum of £________/ for the reason that *(give reason/s)*

2 *I AWARD AND DIRECT* that the *(Party)* do pay forthwith to the *(Party)* the sum of £________ *(amount in words also)* / *together with* an additional sum in respect of interest thereon to be calculated at the rate of *(rate)* per centum per annum from *(date)* to and including the date of this my Award / in full and final settlement of all claims and counter-claims referred to me as aforesaid (Q) (R)

3 *AND I FURTHER AWARD AND DIRECT* that the *(Party)* bear and pay his own and the *(Party/s)* costs in the arbitration (to be taxed on a *(Scale)* basis if not agreed) and that the *(Party)* bear and pay the / charges of *(Administering authority)* / costs of this my Award / which I hereby tax and settle at £________ *(amount in words)* inclusive of my fees and expenses / and Value Added Tax thereon at the rate of *(Rate)* per centum (S) (T)

13 *ALWAYS PROVIDED* that if the *(Party)* shall have paid all or any of the costs of this my Award he shall forthwith be reimbursed by the *(Party)* the full amount so paid

14 Fit for Counsel (U)

Given under my hand the day/year first above written

....

(Arbitrator in the above matter)

In the presence of:

(Signature) .... (V)

(Address)

(Designation)

Notes

(A) This heading incorporates the 1975 Act; see Note (A) in (1) (p. 122).
(B) Insert name of Body (if any) whose Rules govern the arbitration proceedings; otherwise, omit this line.
(C) Name/address of Claimant.
(D) Name/address of Respondent.
(E) Insert date of principal Agreement.
(F) Describe role/obligations of Claimant under principal Agreement.
(G) As for (F) but in respect of Respondent.
(H) The arbitration provisions of the principal Agreement must be stated precisely as expressed therein – the typical wording used in the example is for illustration only; alternatively, the arbitration clause in the principal Agreement may be quoted verbatim or the arbitration agreement could be incorporated by reference and annexed to the Award.
(I) Insert name of nominating authority, if any.
(J) Define the Rules and/or insert name of administering authority; this may or may not be the same as the nominating authority – see arbitration agreement.
(K) Insert only as/when appropriate.
(L) Adapt according to whether the parties appeared in person or were represented by advocates.
(M) Adapt according to whether or not there was an inspection.
(N) Summarise the Claimant's claims.
(O) Summarise the Respondent's counter-claim/s, if any.
(P) The typical wording used in the example is for illustration only; if reasons are required to be given for the decisions reached by the arbitrator they can be stated as indicated; in doing so, it is suggested that such Reasons *(but not 'Reasoning')* be stated as cogently/briefly as possible.
(Q) This is the (net) amount due and payable after allowing for any successful counter-claim.
(R) The award of interest as an addition to the principal amount is an option but, in most cases, the best way to deal with any interest allowable up to the date of the award may be to include it in the calculation which results in the amount stated. In doing so, consideration can be given, subject to legal advice if necessary, to the question of compounding the interest which would otherwise have accrued over the relevant period.
(S) State scale for basis of taxation; usually, a 'Party-and-Party' basis should be appropriate.
(T) The reference to an 'administering authority' is applicable only to administered arbitrations.
(U) The reference to Counsel is appropriate only when the parties or either of them is represented by Counsel *and* the arbitrator considers that such representation was justified in the circumstances.
(V) The arbitrator's signature should be attested.

(14) Award (General): Short Form

In the matter of the Arbitration Acts 1950 to 1979
and
in the matter of an arbitration
under the rules of *(Body)*
between *(Name)*
of *(Address)* – Claimant

and *(Name)*
of *(Address)* – Respondent

THIS IS THE FINAL AWARD of me (Full names of arbitrator) of (address)
made and published in (Town/City) *the* *day of* *19*

1 *WHEREAS* – on the day of 19 an Agreement was entered into between the above named Parties whereby the *(Party)* undertook to *(describe obligations)* and the *(Party)* undertook to *(describe obligations)*

2 *AND* – the said Agreement incorporates, *inter alia,* the following clause (hereinafter referred to as 'the arbitration clause') –
(Here set out the arbitration clause)

3 *AND* – a dispute having arisen between the said Parties on the said Agreement the *(Party)* applied on *(Date)* to the President of *(Body)* for the nomination of an Arbitrator as provided in the said arbitration clause

4 *AND* – the said President nominated me, *(Full names of arbitrator),* for appointment as sole Arbitrator to hear and determine the said dispute and I accepted such appointment

5 *AND* – the Parties agreed that the Arbitration be conducted under the Rules of *(Body)*

6 *Now I, the said* *(Full names of arbitrator)* *do hereby find*

and hold / by consent of the parties / that the Claimant / succeeds / fails / in his claim for *(state nature of claim)* / in the sum of £_________ *(amount in words)*

7 *And I adjudge and award* that the / Respondent / Claimant / pay forthwith to the / Claimant / Respondent / the sum of £_________ *(amount in words)* in full and final settlement of all claims and counter-claims in the Reference

8 *I also award and direct* that the / Respondent / Claimant / bear and pay his own and the / Claimant's / Respondent's / costs to be taxed on a party-and-party basis if not agreed

9 *And I further direct* that the *(Party)* bear and pay the costs of this my Award which I hereby tax and settle at £_________ *(amount in words)* inclusive of my fees and expenses / and Value Added Tax at the current standard rate

Given under my hand the day/year first above written

....
(Arbitrator in the above matter)

In the presence of:
(Signature) ....
(Address)

(Designation)

Notes

The Notes in (13) (p. 149) should be referred to and applied as appropriate.

(15) Special Case Procedure Under the 1950 Act

Until it was abolished by S.1 of the 1979 Act, the 'case stated' or 'special case' procedure was an almost unique factor in arbitration proceedings under the English system. Until then, S.21 of the Arbitration Act 1950 had provided that:

1 an arbitrator may (and, if so directed by the High Court, must) state a special case for the decision of the High Court in respect of any questions of law arising in the proceedings and/or an award or any part thereof;
2 such special case may (or, if so ordered, shall) be referred to the High Court at any time during the proceedings;
3 the High Court's decision on a case stated is subject to appeal provided that no such appeal can be made about any such decision on a point of law without leave.

That procedure was the means whereby an arbitrator could or, in certain circumstances, had to request a decision of the court on a question of law before his award was either made or implemented. The process was initiated at the option of the arbitrator – nudged, perhaps, by one or both of the parties – or he could be directed to do so by the court upon application by one or more of the parties. The arbitrator could not thus seek guidance about the facts of the case; the procedure was exclusively concerned with questions of law which, in practice, were usually related to the proper construction of the relative documents and/or the application of the law to the facts as found, or could be found, by the arbitrator. Thereby the legal rights and obligations of the parties could be established under the particular agreement which governed their relationship within the framework of the English law.

During a debate in the House of Lords in May 1978 it was pointed out that the case stated procedure was a deterrent to foreign parties having arbitrations heard in London. It was said that lawyers in America and elsewhere were advising clients not to invoke English arbitration and the reasons for this, it was alleged, were related to the facility provided by the case stated procedure for delay by a party who wished to take undue advantage of the opportunity for doing so. Consequently, it was argued, parties to international contracts should have the power to opt in (or out) of the provisions of S.21 of the 1950 Act. Other desirable reforms mentioned in the debate included suggestions that there be a separate category for maritime insurance and commodity market contracts, that in certain circumstances arbitrators should be required to give reasons for their decisions, that the court should be given power to order the 'consolidation' of parallel or similar proceedings, that means be devised to avoid abuses of the case stated procedure and that the right of appeal on a point of law should be only by leave of the court. These and other aspects of the arbitration system were the subject of *'Report on Arbitration'* issued by the Commercial Court Committee in advance of the House of Lords debate.

In replying to that debate, the Lord Chancellor (Lord Elwyn Jones) promised his sympathetic consideration of the matters raised in the debate and in the report by the Commercial Court Committee. Subsequently, under the provisions of the 1979 Act, the 'special case' procedure was replaced by a limited right of appeal to the court on points of law.

It seems probable that arbitration proceedings initiated before the 1979 Act became effective may continue for some time and the following details are mentioned for the benefit of those who may be involved in such cases and others whose interest may be academic or historic.

Under S.21 of the 1950 Act, a special case on a question of law could be 'stated' during the course of a reference or it could be incorporated in an Award. In other words, a case could be stated with regard to any question of law which arose during the arbitration proceedings, or with regard to the legal aspects of an Award or any part of it. The procedure could also be relevant to an interim Award or any part of it.

Thus, it is possible to identify two types of special case: firstly, a 'consultative case' – when the arbitrator sought the guidance of the court before his Award was published; secondly, an 'award case' – when the arbitrator made his Award or some part of it in the form of a special case. The ensuing decision of the court was a judgment of the court within S.27 of the Supreme Court of Judicature (Consolidation) Act 1925. In practice, it appears that only in a relatively small proportion of the total number of award cases did the parties incur the extra expense of referring the matter to the court – preferring, instead, to reach agreement between themselves in the light of the arbitrator's findings. Among the reasons for this is the clarification of the position as expressed in such findings even though they are made subject to a ruling by the court on the specific question/s stated.

In any case, it should be noted that there was no appeal from a decision of the court on a question of law raised by a consultative case unless the court or the Court of Appeal gave special permission. In an award case there was an automatic right of appeal without such leave. Although the proportion of all award cases which eventually came before the High Court can never be ascertained precisely, such appeals were not uncommon and several important issues decided by the Court of Appeal and the House of Lords first appeared in the courts as cases stated by arbitrators or as motions by parties seeking to upset an arbitrator's award or to reverse a judgment in special case proceedings.

Typical submission under special case procedure

See Notes below

In the matter of the Arbitration Act 1950
and
in the matter of an arbitration
between *(Name)* – Claimant
and *(Name)* – Respondent

SPECIAL CASE stated under Section 21 of the Arbitration Act 1950 for the decision of the Court.

1 By an Agreement dated *(Date)* (a certified true copy of which is identified by reference *(Ref)* and attached hereto) between the above named Claimant ('the Contractor') and Respondent ('the Employer') the Claimant agreed to execute and complete *(describe the Works)* for which the Respondent agreed to pay the sum of *(Contract Sum)* or such other sum as should be ascertained as provided in the said Agreement.

2 I find the following facts:

(a) during the early months of 1963 the execution of the Works was properly suspended for thirteen weeks because of the adverse effect of sub-zero atmospheric temperatures,

(b) subject as provided under Clause 23 of the said Agreement, the Contractor is entitled to an extension of time in respect of any period during which the completion of the Works is likely to be delayed by, inter alia, exceptionally inclement weather.

(c) the Contractor gave due notice accordingly and the Architect duly extended the time for the completion of the Works by eleven weeks. In doing so, he allowed for a two-week period of 'normally inclement' weather and extended the Contract time by the period he thus assessed as being 'exceptionally inclement'.

Now, therefore, the question for the court is –

Whether in the stated circumstances, the contract period should be extended by thirteen weeks or by eleven weeks or by some other period.

And this I respectfully submit

....

(Arbitrator in the above Matter)

Notes

(a) The same sort of question could now be submitted, subject to the provisions of the 1979 Act, by modifying the heading in the above format as follows:

In the matter of the Arbitration Acts 1950 and 1979

QUESTION OF LAW submitted under Section 2 of the Arbitration Act 1979 for the decision of the Court.

(b) Such submission is made –
(1) by (or on behalf of) a party with the consent of the arbitrator, or,
(2) by (or on behalf of) all parties.

(c) Obviously, no such submission can be made when the parties have made an 'exclusion agreement' under S.3 of the 1979 Act.

(d) In any case, the Court may refuse such application unless it satisfies the criteria defined in S.2(2) of that Act.

Bibliography

The following publications are among those from which additional information may be obtained:

1 General Law and Practice

Bickley, *Little Red Book of Bristol,* Bristol Corporation, 1900
Veale, (ed.), *Great Red Book of Bristol,* 5 vols, Bristol Record Society, 1931–53
Seabrooke, *Evidence,* (Nutshell Series), Sweet & Maxwell, London 1981
Newton, *General Principles of Law,* Sweet & Maxwell, London 1977
Tyas, *Law of Torts,* (M & E Handbook Series), MacDonald & Evans, London 1968
Salmond and Heuston, *Law of Torts (Salmond),* Sweet & Maxwell, London 1981
Elliot, *Manual of the Law of Evidence (Phipson),* Sweet & Maxwell, London 1980
Redmond, *General Principles of English Law,* MacDonald & Evans, London 1981
Casson and Dennis, *Pleading and Practice (Odgers),* Stevens, London 1981
Whitbourn, *The Lawyer's Remembrancer,* Butterworths, London 1983

2 Arbitration: Commercial Disputes (Domestic)

Martin Domke, 'Arbitration' in *Encyclopaedia Britannica,* (15th Edition), London 1983
Rodgers, *The Encyclopaedia of Forms and Precedents, vol 2: Arbitration,* Butterworths, London (4th Edition)
Pearson, in Pieter Saunders (ed.) *Arbitration and the Business Man: Liber Amicorum for Martin Domke,* Martinus Nijhoff, The Hague 1967
Walton, *Arbitration (Russell),* Stevens & Sons, London 1982

Walton, 'Arbitration' in *Halsbury's Laws of England*, vol. 2, Butterworths, London (4th Edition)
Fry, *Official Referee's Business*, Stevens & Sons, London 1983
Parris, *The Law and Practice of Arbitrations*, Godwin, London 1974
Gill, *The Law of Arbitration*, Sweet & Maxwell, London 1983
Parris, *Casebook of Arbitration Law*, Godwin, London 1976
Gibson-Jarvie/Hawker, *A Guide to Commercial Arbitration Under the 1979 Act*, C.I.Arb, London 1980
Kay, *Arbitration* (Essential Business Law Series), Sweet & Maxwell, London 1980
Lord-Smith, *Arbitration for Builders*, Northwood, London 1980
Stephenson, *Arbitration for Contractors*, Northwood, London 1982
Mustill and Boyd, *The Law and Practice of Commercial Arbitration in England*, Butterworths, London 1982
RIBA, *The Architect as Arbitrator*, RIBA Publications, London 1978
ICE, *Arbitration Procedure (1983)*, Thomas Telford, London 1983
CIArb, *Arbitration* (Journal) and Other Publications
Parris, *Arbitration, Principles and Practice*, Granada, London 1983
RICS, *Guidance Notes for Surveyors Acting as Arbitrators or as Independent Experts in Rent Reviews*, 2nd edition, September 1983, Surveyors Publications

3 Arbitration: Commercial Disputes (International)

International Council for Commercial Arbitration, Sanders (ed.), *Yearbooks: Commercial Arbitration*, Kluwer B.V., Netherlands (from 1976)

4 Arbitration: Trade Disputes

Arbitration, Conciliation and Mediation in Trade Disputes (pamphlet), ACAS 1983
Williams and Walker, *Industrial Tribunals – Practice and Procedure*, Butterworths, London 1980
Lockyer, *Industrial Arbitration in Great Britain*, Institute of Personnel Management, London 1980
Wright, *Labour Law* (M & E Handbook Series), MacDonald & Evans, London 1981
Walton, *New Encyclopaedia of Employment Law and Practice*, Centurion Publications, regularly updated

King, *The Application of Arbitration Practice in Industrial Relations,* Paper at Meeting of I.Arb., 22 March 1963
ACAS, *Annual Reports* and Other Publications

5 Arbitration Rules: published by:

Chartered Institute of Arbitrators (CIArb)
London Court of International Arbitration (LCIA)
International Chamber of Commerce (ICC)
United Nations Commission on International Trade Law (UNCITRAL)

6 Contract

Guest (ed.), *Chitty on Contracts,* Sweet & Maxwell, London 1983
Wallace, *Building and Engineering Contracts (Hudson),* Sweet & Maxwell, London 1970 with 1979 supplement
Keating, *Building Contracts,* Sweet & Maxwell, London 1978 with 1982 supplement
Uff, *Construction Law,* Sweet & Maxwell, London 1982
Smith and Thomas, *A Casebook on Contract,* Sweet & Maxwell, London 1982
Turner, *Building Contracts: a Practical Guide,* George Godwin, London 1983
Diamond *et al. Sutton and Shannon on Contracts,* Butterworths, London 1980
CIoB, *Contracts and Building Law: a Review of the Literature,* Chartered Inst. of Building, London 1970–76 (vol. 1), 1977–80 (vol. 2)
Furmeston and Cheshire, *Fifoot's Law of Contract,* Butterworth's, London 1981
Walker-Smith and Close, *The Standard Forms of Building Contract,* Charles Knight, London/Tonbridge 1971 with supplements 1–7
Parris, *The Standard Form of Building Contract, JCT 80,* Granada, London 1982
Powell-Smith and Sims, *Building Contract Claims,* Granada, London 1983

7 Court Procedure

Supreme Court Practice (The White Book)
Gregory, *The County Court Practice (The Green Book),* Butterworths, London 1983

Williams, *ABC Guide to Practice of the Supreme Court,* Sweet & Maxwell, London 1981
Williams, *ABC Guide to Practice of the County Court,* Sweet & Maxwell, London 1982
Birks, *Small Claims in the County Court,* Lord Chancellor's Department 1982
Suing on Your Own, Lord Chancellor's Department 1981
Fay, *Official Referees' Business,* Sweet & Maxwell, London, 1983

8 Dictionaries/Directories

Cunningham, *A New and Complete Law Dictionary,* H.M. Law Printers, London 1764
Burke, *Concise Law Dictionary (Osborn),* Sweet & Maxwell, London 1983
Jowitt, *Dictionary of English Law,* Sweet & Maxwell, London 1977 with 1981 supplement
Stroud, *Judicial Dictionary of Words and Phrases,* Sweet & Maxwell, London 1982
Halsbury's Laws of England, Butterworths, London (4th Edition)
Saunders, *Words and Phrases Legally Defined,* Butterworths, London 1977
Henderson, *Directory of British Associations,* CBD Research, Beckenham 1972
Walker, *The Oxford Companion to Law,* Clarendon, Oxford 1980
Millard, *Trade Associations and Professional Bodies of the United Kingdom,* Pergamon, Oxford 1971

9 Consumer and Other Publications

Cole and Diamond, *The Consumer and the Law,* Co-operative Union, Loughborough 1960
Borrie and Diamond, *The Consumer, Society and the Law,* Penguin Books, Harmondsworth 1964
Gundrey, *At Your Service,* Penguin Books, Harmondsworth 1964
Watson, *Nothing but the Truth,* Estates Gazette, London 1971
Little, *The Ouzel Galley,* Cahill, Dublin 1973
Wagner, *Barnardo,* Weidenfeld and Nicolson, London 1979
Mildred, *The Expert Witness,* George Godwin, London 1982
Sundry other publications by professional bodies, trade associations, trade unions and consumer-protection agencies.

10 Official Publications, etc

Statutes

Statute of Limitations 1623
Articles of Regulation 1695
Arbitration Act 1698
Court of Session (Scotland) Act 1850
Common Law Procedure Act 1854
Civil Procedure Act 1883
Arbitration Act 1889
Sale of Goods Act 1893
Merchant Shipping Act 1894
Arbitration (Scotland) Act 1894
Conciliation Act 1896
Industrial Court Act 1919
Arbitration Clauses (Protocol) Act 1924
Arbitration (Foreign Awards) Act 1930
London Building Act 1930
Administration of Justice (Scotland) Act 1933
Arbitration Act 1934
Arbitration Act (Northern Ireland) Act 1937
Limitation Act 1939
London Building Acts (Amendment) Act 1939
Agricultural Holdings Act 1948
Criminal Justice Act 1948
Legal Aid and Advice Act 1949
Lands Tribunal Act 1949
Arbitration Act 1950
Administration of Justice Act 1953
Tribunals and Enquiries Act 1958
County Courts Act 1959
Consumer Protection Act 1961
Limitation Act 1963
Contracts of Employment Act 1963
Legal Aid Act 1964
Hire Purchase Act 1965
Trade Descriptions Act 1968
Civil Evidence Act 1968
Administration of Justice Act 1970
Consumer Protection Act 1971
Tribunals and Enquiries Act 1971
Civil Evidence Act 1972
Contracts of Employment Act 1972

Administration of Justice (Scotland) Act 1972
Fair Trading Act 1973
Administration of Justice Act 1973
Supply of Goods (Implied Terms) Act 1973
Legal Aid Act 1974
Consumer Credit Act 1974
Trade Union and Labour Relations Act 1974
Employment Protection Act 1975
Courts Act 1975
Arbitration Act 1975
Sex Discrimination Act 1975
Limitation Act 1975
Restrictive Trade Practices Act 1976
Race Relations Act 1976
Administration of Justice Act 1977
Unfair Contract Terms Act 1977
Sale of Goods Act 1979
Arbitration Act 1979
Estate Agents Act 1979
Competition Act 1980
Supreme Court Act 1981
Administration of Justice Act 1982

Statutory rules and orders and statutory instruments

See Official List

Law reports

Authentic reports of the judgments in particular cases can be seen in one or more of the following publications:

The Times Law Reports (TLR), *The Times*, London
The All England Law Reports (AER), Butterworths, London
Weekly Law Reports (WLR), Council for Law Reporting, London
Lloyds Law Reports (Lloyd's Rep) Lloyds of London
Building Law Reports (BLR), George Godwin, London

Glossary of Relevant Words and Phrases

The following are 'working definitions' of some of the terms and phrases which are likely to be met by those concerned in arbitration and related matters.

Further and more comprehensive definitions are contained in standard works such as those mentioned in the Bibliography.

ACA Association of Consultant Architects.

ACAS Advisory, Conciliation and Arbitration Service. Established under S.1 of the Employment Protection Act 1975.

Act Act of Parliament; Statute. Sometimes referred to, shortly, by the year of enactment; for example – 'the 1950 Act' for the Arbitration Act 1950.

Act of God An irresistible super-human event (e.g. storm, tempest, flood)

Action Proceedings in a civil court.

Ad idem 'Of one mind'.

Adjudication A Decision; Judgment (in court) or Award (in arbitration).

Administered Arbitration See **Arbitration–Administered.**

Administering Body The Body or Service designated to administer the arbitration proceedings when so provided in the relative agreement.

Admission Acknowledgement that a statement or other submission is correct.

Affidavit A written statement identifying documents or setting down facts, figures and (sometimes) the opinion which a particular person (the **Deponent**) puts forward and 'swears' as to its veracity before a Public Notary (Commissioner for Oaths). Not generally used in Scotland.

Affirmation See **Oath-taking.**

Agent One who is specifically authorised to act on behalf of another.

ALL ER All England Law Reports.

Amiable Compositeur A function permitted by the laws of some countries whereby arbitrators can settle disputes 'in justice and fairness'

– without the strict application of law but within the limitations of **Public Policy.**

Amicus Curiae 'Friend of the Court'; Counsel not representing a party in a particular case but invited or allowed by the court to assist the proceedings by adducing evidence and/or argument related to the public interest (see **Public Policy**) or to the interests of a party or parties who may be affected by but not directly involved in the issues in question.

Animus Intention; Mental impulse.

Appeal The process of taking a matter to a higher court – usually, of course, in the hope that a decision by the lower court will be reversed or otherwise modified. With certain exceptions, appeals can be made only by leave of the Court.

Application Submission by a party requesting an arbitrator or judge to make or vary an order of directions or to permit a particular course of action.

Arbitrage Dealings in foreign currency, Bills of Exchange or Stocks for commercial gain. Nothing to do with arbitration.

Arbitration Procedure whereby a dispute is referred to and decided by an independent person or tribunal whose decision the parties have bound themselves to accept. In this book, unless otherwise indicated, the term is applied to 'commercial arbitration'.

Arbitration–Administered Arbitration proceedings in respect of which the arbitrator is supported by an administration service which relieves him of some of the 'mechanics' without interfering with his over-all responsibilities and independence.

Arbitration – ***Ad Hoc*** Arbitration proceedings in which the arbitrator/s and/or umpire act/s independently under the terms of the **Arbitration Agreement.**

Arbitration – Domestic An arbitration between parties who are (or deemed to be) resident in the same State and within the jurisdiction of the courts of that State.

Arbitration – Institutional Arbitration proceedings in respect of which the supporting administration service is provided by a designated body in accordance with the provision incorporated in the relative **Arbitration Agreement.**

Arbitration – International An arbitration which includes a **Foreign Element.**

Arbitration Agreement An agreement to refer disputes for adjudication by any person/s other than a court of competent jurisdiction. By such agreement the parties commit themselves to refer to arbitration any dispute defined therein or otherwise embraced thereby and, consequently, come within the provisions of the Arbitration Acts.

Arbitrator/Arbiter A person who has jurisdiction (alone or as a member of a board or tribunal) to hear and determine a dispute referred to arbitration.

Attestation A signed statement by one person which authenticates the signature of another person on the same document.

Award An arbitrator's decision, given in writing, by which the matters in dispute are determined. Interim Awards can be issued when, for example, the arbitrator wishes to publish his decision on certain issues while reserving his position with regard to others; to that extent, an interim award is as binding and enforceable as any (final) award.

Award – Convention See **Convention Award.**

Award – Foreign See **Foreign Award.**

Award – Non-Speaking An award which does not express the reason/s for its decision/s. Sometimes said to be 'non-motivated'.

Bill of Costs An account – setting out details of the costs and charges incurred by a party arising in connection with proceedings.

Breach of Contract Non-compliance with the terms or any substantive provision of a legally enforceable contract – thereby exposing the defaulting party to liability for damages.

Bundle An appropriately labelled and identified batch of correspondence and/or other documents in which the contents are numbered consecutively for ease of reference in arbitration or litigation proceedings – especially at the hearing.

Burden of Proof Onus of proof. A party who makes an allegation must prove its veracity; it is not for the other party to disprove such allegation.

By Consent By mutual agreement by and between the parties.

CASEC Committee of Associations of Specialist Engineering Contractors.

Case Law See **Common Law.**

Case Stated See **Special Case.**

CAT Court of Appeal Transcript/s.

Cause of Action Legal (as distinct from moral) grounds for complaint.

CAV *Curia Advisari Vult;* Reserved judgment.

Caveat Warning.

Caveat Emptor 'Let the buyer beware'; he buys 'as it is'.

CCR County Court Rules.

Certiorari Power vested in a superior court to nullify and/or rectify the decision of a lower court or other tribunal in order to ensure that justice is done under the law.

Charter Party A contract (agreement) between ship-owner and merchant-trader whereby a ship (or part of its capacity) is hired for a particular voyage or period of time.

CIArb Chartered Institute of Arbitrators.

CIF Cost, Insurance and Freight. When goods are sold 'CIF' the seller is responsible for their being supplied, shipped, insured and delivered at the specified destination – and for obtaining and forwarding the relative documents to the buyer.

Civil Action Legal proceedings initiated by one civilian against another – seeking a remedy in damages under Civil Law.

Claim Statement of what is alleged to be lawfully due. In the High Court this is headed **Statement of Claim;** in the County Court the corresponding term is **Plaint.**

Claimant/Respondent In arbitration proceedings, the Claimant is equivalent to the **Plaintiff** in a law suit; i.e. the party who initiates proceedings.

The other party in arbitration proceedings is the **Respondent** – equivalent to the **Defendant** in litigation.

Commercial Court A court within the Queens Bench Division of the High Court set up specially to deal with commercial disputes. Submissions arising from commercial arbitration proceedings and any related applications by the parties thereto are normally dealt with by the commercial court at first instance.

Common Law The system of English law which has emerged as a result of the decisions of the courts in civil actions from time immemorial; sometimes referred to as **Case Law.**

Community Law Statutory enactments by the European Economic Community (EEC) established by the Treaty of Rome, signed on 25 March 1957 and effective from 1 January 1958. The UK became a full member in 1973.

Conciliation A process whereby parties are persuaded to reach a mutually agreed (but legally non-binding) solution of the dispute between them.

Condition An essential term of an agreement or contract which, if broken, destroys the fundamental intention of the parties as therein expressed; it amounts to **Repudiation** which can expose the repudiator to an action for breach of contract – a civil (not criminal) offence.

Conference Consultation between solicitor and counsel with, sometimes, one or more experts in attendance. A party, as such, may be also present at a particular conference.

Consideration Something promised by one party to a contract which is of value (money or money's-worth) and given or surrendered in exchange for the supply of goods and/or services or for something done or not done or given up by one party for the benefit of the other.

Construction Legal interpretation of a document or the distillation of the combined purport of two or more documents embodied in a particular agreement.

Consumer A customer who purchases goods and/or services and who does NOT do so as a transaction in connection with any trade or business with which he/she is associated. (See S.12 of the Unfair Contract Terms Act 1977.)

Contra Proferentem A general legal principle whereby, in the event of ambiguity in the provisions of a document, the benefit of any doubt is given in favour of the party who did not initiate the incorporation of such document in the relevant contract.

Contract A legally enforceable agreement between two or more parties.

Convention Practice based on agreed method of procedure. In the sphere of international arbitration, the term refers to one of the international agreements whereby an award issued in one participating State can be enforced in another.

Convention Award An award under an arbitration agreement with a foreign element made in a State which is a party to the 1958 New York Convention.

Costs Expenses incurred by a party in preparing and presenting his case and/or defending himself against a claim against him in litigation or arbitration proceedings.

Costs – Party-and-Party Scale The basic scale of allowable costs in a court action assessed on the minimum amount of expenditure which is deemed to be reasonably necessary for the enforcement or defence of a party's rights; this is the scale usually specified in an arbitrator's award.

Costs – Solicitor-and-Client Scale A similar High Court scale which allows higher charges than on the Party-and-Party scale and is sometimes referred to as the 'common fund basis'. This includes all fees and expenses incurred by a solicitor's client in preparing and pursuing his case through the courts to the extent that they are reasonably and properly so incurred.

Costs to Follow the Event 'Loser pays all, or most, of the costs of both parties'. When this is stated by a judge or arbitrator, the costs of the party who wins the case will be payable, subject to certain limits, by the other party.

Counter-Claim See **Pleadings.**

County Court A local court, operating under the County Courts Act 1959, presided over by a Judge and administered by a Registrar.

Court The High Court – unless otherwise indicated. The ascending order of jurisdiction/competence of the Courts in civil actions is –

(a) the **County Court** (CC)
(b) the **High Court** (HC)
(c) the **Court of Appeal** (CA)
(d) the **House of Lords** (HL)

Cross-Examination The examination of a **Witness** at a **Hearing** by or on behalf of the party opposed to the party by whom such witness is called to testify.

Damage Any loss, disadvantage or injury suffered by anyone as a consequence of the act or neglect of another.

Damages The amount held to be payable by or on behalf of the person who causes personal injury or other **Damage** to the one who has suffered it.

Damages: Derisory/Exemplary The court or an arbitrator may award a nominal (Derisory) amount as **Damages** when, for example, a party wins the judgment or award on a technicality but leaves the tribunal convinced that his claim and/or the manner of pursuing it was not reasonable in the particular circumstances; in addition, such party may be ordered to bear his own costs and, even, to pay some or all of the other party's costs.

In other circumstances, the court (but not an arbitrator) may order that an extra sum be included in the measure (amount) of **Damages** – thereby punishing the defaulter and discouraging others from doing the same; the amount thus payable is said to be **Exemplary Damages.**

Damages: Liquidated/Ascertained The amount held to be payable by or on behalf of the person who causes personal injury or other **Damage** to the one who has suffered it. Some contracts stipulate the amount to be paid as damages in the event of non-compliance – or, instead, prescribe a formula by means of which such sums would be calculated.

Such amount is termed **Liquidated and Ascertained Damages** and must be capable of being shown to be a reasonable pre-estimate of the damage likely to be suffered; as such, it is automatically payable or allowable once the liability to pay has been established.

Damnum Sine Injuria **Damage** in respect of which there is no legal liability for **Damages.**

Date-Table Schedule of dates set out in an **Order of Directions** to regulate the pace of the proceedings.

Daywork Construction works/services for which payment is made on the basis of the relative expenditure of time, materials, plant, equipment and other items involved.

De Bene Esse Provisionally; In anticipation of possibility that it may be required later (by when it may not be obtainable).

Declaration See **Oath-Taking.**

Deed A written agreement duly 'signed, sealed and delivered' by the parties; such agreements need not incorporate a **Consideration.**

Defence Reply to a claim or counter-claim stating why, in the opinion of the defender, such claim/counter-claim should be rejected.

Defendant The party against whom the (major) claim is made in **Litigation** proceedings. In arbitrations and in cases before the **Court of Appeal** the Defendant is referred to as **Respondent.**

Deponent A person who makes a written statement (affidavit) and swears to the truth thereof before a Commissioner for Oaths (or a magistrate in criminal cases).

Deposition A document so sworn by a **Deponent.**

Derisory Damages See **Damages: Derisory/Exemplary.**

Dictum A statement made by a judge in giving judgment. *Obiter Dictum* is a comment by a judge which is not germane to the matter/s on trial and, therefore, has no significance in **Case Law.**

Directions Orders issued by a judge or an arbitrator to govern the conduct of proceedings.

Discovery A legal term meaning Disclosure for inspection.

Disqualification The grounds on which a person may be disqualified from acting as arbitrator in a particular case include his inability to act judicially and impartially by virtue of the fact that he is biased or has personal or financial interests in any individual or matter in the dispute. He could also become disqualified by **Misconduct.**

Document Originally, anything on which something is written which may be relevant to the matter/s in dispute. Now, in addition to correspondence and contract agreements, the term embraces such other items as plans, technical specifications, telex messages, tape recordings, electronically processed data; it could also include the inscription on a memorial tablet or tomb-stone.
See also **Exhibit.**

Domestic Within the UK.

Domicile The place where a person resides or where a company has its registered address.

Duces Tecum See *Subpoena Duces Tecum.*

Duress Violence, or other sanction, or threat thereof, intended to compel a person to do something against his wishes.

Estoppel The principle which 'stops' an intended process. For example, a party may be 'estopped' when trying to establish in legal proceedings that some fact previously established and acted upon was not what it then appeared to be. Such 'facts' may have been established by (1) the findings of a court or other tribunal, or (2) a deed to which the party concerned has set his seal, or (3) the word or conduct of a party by which another is reasonably entitled to act on the presumption that the fact in question was as thus represented.

Evidence Information laid before a judge or arbitrator with the object of enabling him to identify and establish the facts of the matter/s in dispute.

Such information may be oral (given in person by a **Witness** at the **Hearing**) or documentary (in a **Document**). By leave, it may also be presented by means of **Affidavit** or on **Commission.**

See also **Witness** and **Judicial Notice.**

Evidence – Circumstantial Evidence of facts which are not in issue but from which a fact in issue may be inferred.

Evidence – Hearsay Repetition by a **Witness** of what he could only have learned from a third party and, as such, not admissible as **Evidence.**

Ex Aequo Et Bono 'In justice and fairness'.

Ex Parte In the absence of a party.

Ex Post Facto After the event.

Examination-in-Chief The examination of a **Witness** at the **Hearing** by or on behalf of the party who calls him to testify. If such witness is further questioned by his side after cross examination by the other side he is thus subjected to **'Re-Examination'.**

See also **Evidence** and **Privilege.**

Exclusion Agreement An agreement – executed on an *ad hoc* basis or expressed as an **Exclusion Clause** in a contract – designed to modify or extinguish certain defined rights or obligations of the parties or any of them under particular Acts or other governing provisions (e.g. the Aribtration Rules of a particular Body) by which they would otherwise be bound.

Such an exclusion agreement can be adopted by the parties when, for example, they wish to exclude the involvement of the courts in accordance with the provisions of S.3 of the 1979 Act. In domestic arbitration proceedings, an exclusion agreement is of no effect with regard to an award or a question of law unless it is made after such proceedings have been commenced.

Execute To do something completely and finally. The term is applied to the drawing-up of a will, agreement or deed, the performance of an obligation, compliance with the terms of a judgment or an **Award** – these being typical of a variety of possible applications.

Executor One charged with the responsibility for ensuring that the terms of a Deed are duly **Executed.**

Executory Something yet to be performed on or by some stipulated date.

Exemplary Damages See **Damages: Derisory/Exemplary.**

Exhibit An object, sample or document exhibited as **Evidence** at the **Hearing.**

Expert A person who is qualified and experienced in the general field in which a dispute has arisen and who has also informed himself about the significant details of a particular dispute.

His role, initially, is to advise the party who engages and pays him for his services; at the **Hearing** his role is to assist the judge or arbitrator in elucidating the facts and coming to a correct view of them.

FASS Federation of Associations of Specialists and Sub-Contractors.

FCEC Federation of Civil Engineering Contractors.

FOB Free on Board (ship). Goods sold 'FOB' become the buyer's property and responsibility once they are loaded at the place of shipment.

Fiduciary Held or given in good faith; on trust. A fiduciary relationship exists, for example, between a solicitor and his client. In any such relationship, the party relied upon must always act in the utmost good faith for the benefit of the other and without gaining any undisclosed benefit for himself by so doing.

Fit for Counsel A statement often incorporated in **Orders** and **Awards** to indicate the **Arbitrator's** opinion that the involvement of Counsel in those matters was justified.

Force Majeure 1 A compelling circumstance.

2 The term has been held to include such contingencies as – capture by enemy forces, threat to safety of a ship or its cargo, complete dislocation of business by, for example, a general strike, delay caused by break-down of machinery, accident to machinery.

3 It has been held not to include – exhausting supplies due to under-estimating requirements, bad weather, football matches, funerals.

Foreign Award In general, an **Award** issued in a Foreign State. In particular, an award to which Part II of the 1950 Act or the 1975 Act applies.

Foreign Element A foreign element exists, for example, when at least one of the parties to an **Arbitration Agreement** belongs to or habitually resides in a **Foreign State.**

It also exists when an **Arbitration Agreement** provides that any proceedings thereunder are conducted in a Foreign State and/or stipulates that the **Proper Law** shall be the law of a Foreign State.

Frustration The situation when a contract becomes incapable of performance because of circumstances beyond the control of either party which arise after the date thereof.

Functus Officio 'Duty done' – and cannot be undone; the legal doctrine that, in effect, an **Arbitrator** 'drops dead' upon signing his **Award.** He cannot re-open the matter (other than to correct minor slips under S.17 of the 1950 Act) unless he is so ordered by the Court.

Further and Better Particulars When statements or other details in the **Pleadings** by one party are thought by the other party to be shallow, evasive or otherwise unsatisfactory, the recipient can ask for 'Further and Better Particulars' in respect of specific matters.

General Damages See **Damages.**

Green Book A standard publication containing the Rules for and general guidance on procedure in County Courts.

Guarantee An undertaking to make good any failure in goods or services to satisfy their intended purpose – subject to certain conditions.

HMSO Her Majesty's Stationery Office – also referred to as the Government Bookshop.

Habeas Corpus: Writs Since Magna Carta (1215) and, particularly, since the famous Habeas Corpus Act 1679, a court may issue a Writ requiring the custodian of a prisoner to bring him/her ('the body') before the court for a specific purpose. As far as the general public is concerned, this process is most often heard of in connection with a writ of *Habeas Corpus ad Subjiciendum* – to show good cause why a prisoner should not be released.

In litigation or arbitration proceedings, if necessary, an application can be made for a writ of *Habeas Corpus ad Testificandum* to be issued by the court – requiring a prisoner to be brought to the **Hearing** in order to testify.

Habeas Corpus, as such, is not part of the Scottish legal system but the same principles are effectively upheld by other enactments.

Hansard The popular term for the official reports of parliamentary proceedings – first supplied by the gentleman of that name.

These reports include in full the proceedings in Parliament –separate volumes being issued in respect of the House of Lords and House of Commons – for every day on which business is conducted.

Hearing The formal hearing by a tribunal of oral submissions, evidence and argument by or on behalf of the parties in dispute.

Hearsay Evidence See **Evidence – Hearsay**

High Court The **High Court** operates in three divisions – the Queen's Bench Division (which includes the Commercial Court and the Admiralty Court), the Chancery Division and the Family Division.

High Court judges sit in the Royal Courts of Justice in London and in provincial circuit centres.

Hostile Witness See **Witness – Hostile.**

House of Lords The highest appeal court in the UK to which, by leave, cases may be referred from all the member countries.

However, under **Community Law,** the European Court of Justice at Luxembourg or the European Court of Human Rights at Strasbourg, may have final jurisdiction in certain matters.

A similar function to that of the House of Lords is performed by the Judicial Committee of the Privy Council in respect of appeals from those overseas territories (one-time UK colonies etc.) which still adhere to that system.

ICC International Chamber of Commerce whose headquarters are in Paris. National/Local headquarters are also maintained in many countries including the UK.

ICE Institution of Civil Engineers.

Indemnity A liability undertaken by one party whereby the obligations or interests of another are under-written.

Industrial Dispute See **Trade Dispute.**

Inspection See **Discovery/Disclosure.**

Institutional Arbitration See **Arbitration – Institutional.**

Interim Award See **Award.**

Interlocutory 'Pre-trial'.

Interlocutory Proceedings Events in the process of preparing a case for trial including, *inter alia,* preliminary submissions, exchange of **Pleadings, Discovery** and **Inspection** of documents and any applications to the tribunal for **Directions.**

Interpleader Proceedings Preliminary proceedings between two parties to settle a point in which a third party is subsequently concerned.

Interrogatory A list of questions sent by one party to another designed to elicit specific information as **Further and Better Particulars.** A convenient format is to set down the questions on the left-hand side of the page, leaving enough space alongside for replies.

IQS Institute of Quantity Surveyors. Merged with the RICS (QS Division) in March 1983.

J Justice (e.g. 'Mr Justice Blank' or 'Blank, J.')

JCT Joint Contracts Tribunal; the oldest recognised authority for the drafting and publication of standard forms of contract and sub-contract for use in connection with the execution of building works.

Joinder The joining of other parties in court proceedings or, when so provided in the respective arbitration agreements, in arbitration proceedings in respect of matters in which such other parties may be involved.

Jointly and Severally Two or more parties standing as a group and, at the same time, as individuals in respect of a particular liability.

Judge-Arbitrator/Umpire A circuit judge of the **Commercial Court** who accepts appointment as sole arbitrator or umpire under an arbitration agreement.

Judgment Debt A sum of money owed by one person to another in accordance with the terms of a Judgment or **Award.**

Judicial Notice Certain well-established facts of common knowledge do not need to be proved when the tribunal has, or is deemed to have, taken Judicial Notice thereof. Otherwise, every fact on which a party relies to establish his case must be proved before the **Tribunal** which hears it.

Jurisdiction The authority of a tribunal and the territory in which such authority can be exercised is the Jurisdiction of a particular tribunal.

LCJ Lord Chief Justice.

LJ Lord Justice.

Law Lord A member of the House of Lords who is also appointed by the Crown as one of the Lords of Appeal in Ordinary or is or has been the holder of the office of Lord Chancellor.

Law Report A fully detailed report by a Barrister of the Judgment/s in selected court cases of general interest.

Legal Aid Financial assistance to parties involved in litigation proceedings under the provisions of the Legal Aid and Advice Act 1949 and subsequent legislation. Such assistance is subject to a 'means test' and is not available to parties involved in arbitration proceedings.

Libel A defamatory publication in written or graphic form. An action for libel may be defended on the grounds that such publication is 'fair comment on a matter of public interest'.

Liberty to Apply Endorsement on an **Order** (other than a **Peremptory Order**) to allow either party to apply for a variation of its terms.

Liberty to Restore Endorsement on an order of the court to permit an application to be made for restoration to the court of proceedings in respect of matters which by that order are noted as being the subject of other proceedings. This provision could be relevant, for example, in an order staying court proceedings under S.4 of the Arbitration Act 1950; it could be also invoked when the matters in dispute, or any of them, have not been otherwise disposed of within a reasonable time.

Lie An action is said to 'lie' when it has been or is thought capable of being successfully prosecuted.

Lien The right to retain possession of goods, documents or other assets as security for the payment of a debt owed by the owner to the one who is holding such goods etc.

Liquidated Damages See **Damages.**

Liquidator A person appointed by shareholders or, in some circumstances, by the court to realise the assets of a company and, after discharging its debts, to distribute the balance (if any) to the shareholders.

Litigation The process of preparing and presenting a case for Judgment in a **Court.**

Locus Standi 'Place of Standing' meaning, in effect, 'right to appear and be heard'.

MR See **Master of the Rolls.**

Man of Straw A person without the financial resources to meet his obligations.

Mandamus A court order compelling a party to perform some specific obligation subject, if necessary, to terms.

Master An official of the High Court acting as a junior judge in dealing with **Interlocutory** matters in Chambers.

Master of the Rolls (MR) A historic title given to the senior judge in the Court of Appeal.

Mediation A process whereby non-binding recommendations for the settlement of disputes are made by an independent third-party.

Misconduct The traditional term applied to any act or omission by an arbitrator or umpire which exposes him or his award to the risk of being set aside by the **Court.** A more realistic alternative term could be **Misdirection.**

Misdirection Misdirection of himself or the proceedings by an arbitrator/umpire may include failure to comply with any of the terms of the **Arbitration Agreement** or to deal with all matters referred as well as other obvious failures to observe the rules of natural justice or to maintain strict impartiality.

Mitigation Reduction. A party who suffers loss or damage is required to take all reasonable steps to Mitigate the amount of such loss or damage.

Motion Application for an **Order.**

Mutatis Mutandis 'After making the obviously necessary changes'.

Natural Justice The general principle of what is fair and reasonable or just and equitable; the concept of British justice and fair play which may or may not be specifically expressed in or protected by the Law. It is based on two main principles –

1 no man shall be condemned unheard;
2 no man shall be the judge in his own cause.

Natural Rights The natural rights of every person include **Natural Justice** and freedom under the Law to speak his mind and to worship whom/when/how he chooses as well as to be free from want and fear. These are enshrined, for example, as the 'four freedoms' of the Atlantic Charter (1941) and incorporated in the Universal Declaration of Human Rights adopted by the United Nations on 10 December 1948 as well as in the European Convention on Human Rights of 4 November 1950, expanded on 20 March 1952. The UK is a party to the European

Convention and is currently committed to maintain its enshrined Right of Petition by individuals.

Negligence The failure to exercise such care and skill as the negligent party is under a duty to render towards another party. If there is a contractual relationship between such parties, negligence may lead to an action for breach of **Contract;** if there is no such contractual relationship, an action may be brought in **Tort.** To succeed, therefore, an action for negligence must prove the existence of three basic factors: duty, breach and damage and that the effect of the negligence was foreseeable. In mitigation, it is sometimes pleaded that the injured party is guilty of **'Contributory Negligence'.**

New York Convention, 1958 New York Convention on the Recognition and Enforcement of Foreign Arbitral Awards – adopted by the United Nations Conference on International Commercial Arbitration on 10 June 1958. This is given effect in and between the U.K. and certain other States by the Arbitration Act 1975.

NFBTE National Federation of Building Trades Employers.

Notary Public Person qualified and authorised, *inter alia,* to attest depositions and other legal documents.

Notice Something specifically communicated and/or otherwise deemed to be within the knowledge of a party – who is thus said to be 'on notice'.

Novation The agreed substitution of one party to a contract by another party – who thereupon proceeds to discharge the unfulfilled obligations of the original party.

Oath-taking 1 An Oath in Court is a solemn declaration, in specific terms, made by a **Witness** as a preliminary statement before giving oral evidence before a tribunal – e.g. 'I swear by Almighty God that the evidence I shall give will be the truth, the whole truth and nothing but the truth.'

In doing so, the **Witness** is usually required to hold up a Bible (or other holy book) to add to the solemnity of his **Oath.**

2 Witnesses who for any reason do not wish to swear in the manner indicated may, instead, make a declaratory **Affirmation** – e.g. 'I solemnly and sincerely declare that the evidence I shall give will be the truth, the whole truth and nothing but the truth'.

Obiter Dictum See **Dictum.**

Offer The first ingredient in a valid **Contract** is the Offer made by one party to the other.

Office of Fair Trading (OFT) An agency established under S.1 of the Fair Trading Act 1973 with the duty and power to enforce the legislation related to commercial transactions entered into by a **Consumer.**

Official Receiver A person appointed by the **Court** to manage a company whose financial affairs are prima facie unsatisfactory.

Official Referee (OR) Now obsolete – see **Referee.**

Official Referee's Business Such business as is defined by Rules of Court made under S.15 of the Administration of Justice Act 1956 or otherwise. In practice, such business is mainly concerned with adjudication in disputes (particularly about quantum) arising, for example, on construction contracts.

Official Referee's Schedule See **Scott Schedule.**

Onus of Proof The **Party** or **Witness** who makes a statement in **Evidence** carries the burden of proving it to be correct.

Order: Order of Directions An Order by a judge or arbitrator setting out his Directions as/when necessary to regulate the conduct of the proceedings before and at the **Hearing.**
See also **Peremptory Order.**

Outside Arbitrator Any person (not being the incumbent judge or registrar) appointed under S.92 of the County Courts Act 1959 to act in accordance with Order 19 of the County Court Rules.

Parole Evidence 'Oral evidence'.

Party One of the persons or bodies who have joined in entering into an **Agreement/Contract** *or* who have (been) joined in **Litigation** or **Arbitration** proceedings.

Party-and-Party Costs See **Costs.**

Payment into Court 1 Any sum offered by a **Defendant** and refused by a **Plaintiff** in a **Court** action may be 'paid into court' with denial of liability – in which case the judge is not informed of the existence or amount of such payment. Alternatively, such payment can be made with admission of liability – whereupon the fact and amount will be disclosed in the **Pleadings.** Then, if the amount awarded in the judgment is less than the amount paid-in the **Plaintiff** will be responsible for meeting the **Costs** incurred by extending the proceedings beyond the date of such payment into **Court.**

2 Another reason for paying money into **Court** may be in compliance with an **Order** that the **Plaintiff** makes such payment as **Security For Costs** – to avoid the risk that a vexatious litigant may cause a **Defendant** to incur expense in defending a frivolous claim by someone who proves to be a **Man of Straw.**

3 A corresponding process in arbitration proceedings is by means of a **Sealed Offer.**

Penalty A punitive measure or punishment – not assessed by direct reference to the damage suffered.

Any provision in a commercial contract whereby a **Penalty** (as distinct from **Damages**) is said to become payable by one party to the other is not legally enforceable.

Per Curiam 'By the **Court**'.

Per Incuriam 'By failure of the **Court**'.

Per Procurationem 'For and on behalf of' – usually abbreviated to 'Per Pro' or 'p.p.'

Peremptory 'Final; absolute'.

Peremptory Order An Order endorsed **Peremptory** must be complied with or, in default, proceedings may continue at a time or in such manner as puts a defaulting party at a disadvantage and/or makes him liable for any extra **Costs.**

Perjury Evidence given by a witness on oath (or affirmation) in court or arbitration proceedings who deliberately misleads the tribunal about a critical matter by making an assertion which he knows to be untrue or about which he knows himself to be ignorant.

Piepowder English (corrupted) version of the French 'pieds poudrés' ('dusty feet').

Piepowder Court The jurisdiction exercised by a mediaeval 'law merchant' – one who travelled from place to place (on foot) in order to adjudicate in disputes which arose in connection with commercial transactions – e.g. at fairs and markets.

Plaint A written **Statement of Claim** in County Court proceedings.

Plaintiff The party who in **Litigation** proceedings makes the (major) **Claim.** In arbitration proceedings the corresponding role is defined as **Claimant.**

Plea Reply to an accusation or charge or a submission in **Mitigation.** To make a Plea is to Plead, one who Pleads is a Pleader.

Pleadings A generic term for documents (described in Chapter 5) prepared respectively by and exchanged between parties as part of **Interlocutory Proceedings.**

Point of Law A matter of construction or interpretation of documents or the application of the relevant Law to particular circumstances.

Privilege Privilege may be 'Qualified' or 'Absolute'. In certain situations (e.g. in Parliament or in Court) everything said is **Privileged** and, as such, is protected against any action for defamation. There is some doubt, however, whether anything defamatory said in the course of arbitration proceedings is similarly protected.

Communications between a solicitor and his client in contemplation or pursuance of legal or arbitration proceedings, and related communications with non-professional agents or third-parties, are also privileged and, therefore, not available for inspection by any other party.

Documents which contain details of trade secrets (i.e. patent designs, processes and other 'know-how') may also be held to be privileged in certain circumstances.

Proof of Evidence A written statement prepared by a **Witness** and handed to the **Party** who calls him; it indicates the **Evidence** such witness is prepared to give at the **Hearing.**
See also **Onus of Proof.**

Promise To be legally enforceable, a Promise must be the subject of a **Deed** or, alternatively, incorporated in a valid **Contract** in which such promise is the **Consideration.**

Proper Law The Law of a particular State which is applicable to a particular **Contract** or **Arbitration Agreement.**

Public Policy Public interest; the interests of the Community as judged by weighing any conflicting claims in the scales of **Natural Justice.**

Puisne Judge A lower grade of High Court judge; the status sometimes accorded (by courtesy) to an arbitrator. Under S.2(4) of the Judicature Act 1925, puisne judges of the HC are styled: 'Justices of the High Court'.

Pursuer The Scottish equivalent of **Plaintiff.**

Quantum Amount, Valuation or Assessment.

Quantum Meruit 'What it is worth'.

Queen's Counsel (QC) Senior Barrister promoted to the status of QC and sometimes referred to as 'a Silk' because, as such, he is entitled to wear a gown of that material.

Ratio Decidendi The substantive **Reasons** for a Court's decision.

Reasonableness Whatever one's rights may be, they will inevitably be subject to the test of **Reasonableness** – judged by the assumed standards of the 'reasonable man' or the proverbial 'man on the Clapham omnibus'.

With reference to 'consumer' contracts, some guidelines for the application of the 'reasonableness test' are set out in Schedule 2 of the Unfair Contract Terms Act 1977.

Reasons The **Reasons** for the decision of the Court are always included in the Judgment.

In **Arbitration** proceedings under the 1950 Act it was the practice of **Arbitrators** not to give **Reasons** for their decisions within their **Awards.** As a compromise, some **Arbitrators** have in the past agreed to supply their **Reasons** in a separate document on the understanding that it will not be used in any subsequent proceedings in relation to the relative **Award.**

Now, the Arbitration Act 1979 provides that an arbitrator can be required to state the reasons for his award – either by the parties in advance of his appointment or by the court if and when an appeal makes this necessary.

An **Award** which contains **Reasons** is a **Motivated Award.**

Receiver A person appointed by the shareholders to carry out the same functions as an **Official Receiver.**

Recitals **Preamble** clauses in an **Award** (or other **Document**) rehearsing the facts/events leading up to the substantive contents of such **Document.**

Red Book of Bristol (a) *Little Red Book of Bristol,* (b) *The Great Red Book of Bristol* – being compilations of the ordinances, etc by which, *inter alia,* trading in the city was governed in the 14th, 15th and 16th centuries.

Reduction In Scotland, the **Reduction** of an **Award** is equivalent to its being **Set Aside** by the English Courts.

Re-examination See **Examination-in-Chief.**

Referee A person to whom a dispute is referred; an umpire. In court or arbitration proceedings the term embraces the additional element of 'judicial assessor'. An **Official Referee (OR)** was an experienced barrister of not less than ten years standing whose powers and duties were derived from SS.9 and 10 of the Administration of Justice Act 1956. Now, since that Act was abolished by S.25 of the Courts Act 1975, the erstwhile functions of an OR are discharged by such of the Circuit Judges in the High Court as the Lord Chancellor appoints for that purpose.

See **Official Referee's Business.**

Reference The formal submission of a dispute to **Arbitration.** Sometimes, the term is used as though it had the same meaning as Arbitration Proceedings.

Regiam Majestatem An early Scottish legal treatise – so-called from its opening words.

Reply See **Pleadings.**

Repudiation Denial, by statement or by conduct, of the existence of some fundamental contractual obligation, thereby exposing the repudiator to an action for **Damages.**

Res 'Things'.

Res Ipsa Loquitur 'Things which are self-evident'; matters which are common knowledge or the cause of which is obvious and do not, therefore, need to be 'proved'.

Res Judicata 'Things previously adjudged and settled'.

Respondent See **Claimant/Respondent.**

Restitutio in Integrum Complete restitution – such as to restore a party to an 'as he was' position before entering upon a particular transaction.

RICS Royal Institution of Chartered Surveyors.

Right of Reply The right of the **Claimant** to make the final address to the **Arbitrator** at a **Hearing.** The Claimant also has the right to open at the **Hearing.**

Roman Law Legal system developed within the Roman Empire – the fundamental concepts of which are perpetuated in the Law of many States.

RSC Rules of the Supreme Court – see below.

Rules of the County Court Rules which govern procedure in County Courts – abbreviated to 'CCR'; also referred to as *The Green Book.*

Rules of the Supreme Court The Rules which govern procedure in the High Court – first issued in 1883 'for the just, expeditious and economical disposal of actions'. As such, they are referred to by the initials **RSC.** These rules are issued in a two-volume publication with white covers – hence the popular term *White Book* used for general reference thereto.

Scott **v.** *Avery* **Clause** A clause in an **Agreement** which provides, in effect, that the publication of an **Award** is a condition precedent to the right of further action in Court in respect of any of the matters so agreed to be referred to an **Arbitrator.**

Scott Schedule A multi-column schedule setting out in respective columns the facts/figures/contentions adduced by each party – with a further (blank) column in which the arbitrator may enter his findings. Also known as 'Official Referee's Schedule'.

Sealed Offer Copy of an offer made by one party (and refused by the other) in full settlement of the matter/s in dispute – enclosed in a sealed envelope and handed to an **Arbitrator** or, if appropriate, to the **Administering Body.** This is opened only after the **Arbitrator** has decided the substantive issues and before he has dealt with liability for costs. At that stage his position is analogous to that of a **Judge** when informed about a **Payment into Court.**

Security (For Costs/Fees/Expenses) A Court may order the deposit of money by a party as security for the costs of another party but an **Arbitrator** cannot himself make such order. However, an arbitrator may order a deposit by both parties as security for his own fees/expenses.

Service A Writ or any other **Notice** or related **Document** must be 'served' before it is effective; such service may be effected by handing the Writ (or other **Document**) to the person concerned or, if it is so agreed, to his solicitor or other agent. Alternatively, service may be effected by post – either by registered or recorded mail.

Set Aside If an **Award** is set aside by an **Order** of the Court it (the **Award**) is of no effect. In such circumstances the parties must either start afresh – or reach agreement by mutual consent.

Set-Off The process of reducing the amount of a claim by, for example, the amount of a counter-claim.

Settlement The final discharge of all outstanding obligations by all parties concerned. Alternatively, an agreement defining what the parties or either of them shall pay or perform to achieve such final discharge.

Severally See **Jointly/Severally.**

Slip Rule The power given to judges and arbitrators to correct minor errors in judgments/awards which do not affect the substance of the decision originally published.

This power is given to arbitrators by S.17 of the 1950 Act.

Solicitor Lawyer who has been admitted to the register of the Law Society.

Solicitor-and-Client Costs See **Costs.**

Special Case Submission by an **Arbitrator** to the Court requesting a ruling on a **Point of Law** which is relevant to the proceedings in a particular **Arbitration.** This was provided for by S.21 of the 1950 Act but repealed by the 1979 Act in favour of a limited provision for appeal in certain circumstances. See (15) in Part III.

Special Damages See **Damages.**

Specific Performance The fulfilment by a party of what he promised under the terms and conditions of a contract. An order for specific performance may be made by a judge and, except with reference to transactions in land, by an arbitrator; in practice, this is not usually done when the matter/s complained of are amenable to the 'healing' of **Damages.**

Statement of Claim See **Pleadings: Points of Claim.**

Status Quo (Status Quo Ante) The position existing at a particular time (e.g. *Status quo ante bellum* – 'the position as it was before the war'); in practice, the position of one or more parties before entering on a particular transaction.

Statute An **Act** of Parliament.

Statute Barred An action may be stopped if it is not initiated within the time allowed by the Limitation Acts – whereupon it is said to be 'Statute Barred'.

See **Statutory Limitation.**

Statute Law That part of the Law which derives its authority from **Acts** of Parliament.

Statutory Instrument (SI) The means whereby Ministers of State publish the Orders/Rules/Regulations made in accordance with the powers and duties vested in them by **Acts** of Parliament.

Previously, SI's were published as Statutory Rules and Orders (SR&O).

Statutory Limitation The effect of the Limitation Act 1939 upon the initiation of proceedings. In relation to simple contracts, ('under hand') any such proceedings must be initiated within six years of the date when the cause of the action accrued; in relation to **Deeds** ('under seal') the corresponding period is twelve years.

Actions initiated outside those periods may be **Statute Barred.**

Statutory Rules/Orders See **Statutory Instrument.**

Stay of Proceedings Suspension or adjournment of proceedings to a future date or circumstance.

Striking Out Anything struck out by order of a Court (or **Arbitrator** if so authorised by the court) puts the party concerned back to the position he was in before the matter in question was initiated.

Sub Judice 'The subject of judicial proceedings'. It is generally held to be a Contempt of Court to utter or publish comment about any matter while it is *Sub Judice.*

Submission The placing before a judge or arbitrator of an application, evidence or argument; alternatively, the substance of such submission. This term is sometimes loosely used instead of **Reference.**

Subpoena 'Under threat of penalty'. In practice, a Writ requiring attendance by a particular person at a specified place and time for a particular purpose.

Subpoena Ad Testificandum Subpoena to attend for the purpose of testifying.

Subpoena Duces Tecum Subpoena to attend for the purpose of bringing and/or identifying documents.

Taxation A function of the Court whereby, upon application, **Bills of Cost** may be 'audited' by a **Master** of the Court (Tax Master) to ensure that they are properly made up and within the scales established as 'norms' in respect of the services reasonably engaged and paid for by the parties. Taxation does not interfere with what a party may have to pay for the legal and other services he has engaged; its purpose is to regulate the amount which one party may properly recover from another in respect of such services.

TLR Times Law Report; published by *The Times* newspaper.

Tort A civil wrong inflicted by one person on another to whom he owes a duty of care in the absence of any contractual relationship between them and which is not exclusively the breach of a Trust or other merely equitable obligation.

Tortfeasor A person who inflicts a **Tort** upon another. In so doing, his conduct is said to be **Tortious.**

Trade Dispute A dispute connected with terms and conditions of employment.

Tribunal One or more persons appointed to hear and determine disputes or appeals against the decisions of lower courts or public officers.

Ultra Vires 'Beyond the power/authority'.

Umpire In certain **Arbitration Agreements** it is provided that two **Arbitrators** – one appointed by each party – shall hear and determine the matter/s in dispute and, if such arbitrators fail to agree, that the said matters are thereupon referred to an Umpire (appointed by the **Arbitrators**) who then acts, in effect, as sole **Arbitrator.**

UNCITRAL An acronym for: United Nations Commission on International Trade Law. Model Rules for the conduct of international arbitrations ('the Uncitral Rules') were first adopted by the UN General Assembly in 1958.

Under Hand A document is **Under Hand** when it is merely signed by or on behalf of each party – such signature being **Attested** by a person (not being a party) who also signs the document to that effect.

Under Seal A document may be executed **Under Seal** by being impressed with the official seal of the body concerned and signed by its officers in accordance with its own rules for so doing.

Vis Major **'Act of God'.**

Volenti Non Fit Injuria 'Volunteer may not complain of injury sustained in the process for which he volunteers'.

Want of Prosecution Unreasonable delay.

Warranty A factor in an agreement which, unlike a **Condition,** is not essential to the proper performance of such agreement.

A breach of warranty may lead to a successful claim for **Damages** but not to **Determination** or **Repudiation** by the aggrieved party.

White Book **Rules of the Supreme Court (RSC).**

Without Prejudice Endorsement which may be attached to conversations or correspondence and other documents passing between parties during any negotiations attempting to reach a **Settlement** of matters in difference between them.

Any exchanges so endorsed cannot be produced as evidence of any admission of liability in litigation or arbitration proceedings unless this is so agreed by all parties.

Witness – General A Person who testifies with reference to what he/she has actually seen/heard – sometimes referred to as a **Witness of Fact.**

Witness – Expert A **Witness of Fact** and **Opinion;** see **Expert.**

Witness – Hostile A **Witness** whose evidence is damaging to a party who, therefore, regards him as 'hostile' and is entitled to treat him as such. If a **Witness** called by a party turns hostile he may, by leave of the presiding judge or arbitrator, be treated as a Hostile Witness by the party who called him.

Index

References to words and phrases in the text which also appear in the Glossary are indicated (e.g.): **G**:162. References to the arbitration Acts are by Year and Section followed by page number (e.g.): (**1950**)*S.4*:92. References to specimen documents in Part III are by the sub-number therein, followed by page number (e.g.): (**1**):119.